GOLDFINGER
AND ME

CONTENTS

ACKNOWLEDGEMENTS

Thank you to my two beautiful daughters, and to my dear departed dad. He gave me everything he had. I also would never have been able to write this book without the loving support of my new partner, John, who has made a future possible. Lastly, I want to thank my husband of forty years, John Palmer.

Marnie Palmer

2018

Tom Morgan would like to thank Charlotte Dunlavey, Quita Morgan, Robert Smith, Alex Waite and Mark Beynon.

(Some names of close family members have been amended in the following pages at Marnie's request, in order to protect their privacy.)

PROLOGUE

On 24 June 2015, John Palmer's luck ran out. The underworld kingpin with riches to rival the Queen collapsed on the grass after being blasted six times by a contract assassin lurking in the shadows of his garden.

For his long list of enemies, Palmer's death had been a long time coming. Murders and fatal 'accidents' had wiped out at least twenty criminals and police officers connected to the spectacular Brink's-Mat bullion raid of 1983. Palmer, who melted down and sold the gold, was the one that got away. Dodging the so-called 'Brink's-Mat curse' for thirty years, he masterminded a fraudulent timeshare empire of which his rivals could only dream.

The press nicknamed Palmer 'Goldfinger'; his rivals knew him as 'Teflon John'; and, as his business assets swelled to an estimated £300 million, associates on Tenerife called him 'Timeshare King'. For those he crossed, however, he was Public Enemy No. 1. By the time he was shot, police estimated tens of thousands of people had reason to want him dead.

Palmer started with nothing and rose to the top by living on his wits. He was born into poverty in September 1950, one of seven siblings who often went to bed hungry in their two-bedroom council home in the Birmingham suburb of Solihull. He left school at 15 barely able to read and write, but with a fierce appetite to prove himself.

As a teenager, his prospects were limited to casual roofing work or the odd shift on his brother's market stall. Young John wanted more. He moved down to Bristol and dreamed big. Silver-tongued and cunning, he was a natural entrepreneur. He soon launched a number of businesses, selling second-hand cast-offs, carpets, antiques and eventually bullion. He then hit upon the idea to build a smelter in his back garden to melt down jewellery, cutlery and unwanted scrap.

Life was good. He fell in love with Marnie Ryan, a warm-natured and charismatic young hairdresser with the looks of Brigitte Bardot. They wed in 1975, eventually having two daughters and buying a beautiful Georgian pile near Bath. In the driveway, of course, was the Rolls-Royce.

But Brink's-Mat changed everything. The newspapers called it 'the crime of the century', but in reality, the operation wasn't so well planned. Six men broke into the US security company's warehouse at Heathrow in November 1983, thinking they were about to steal £3 million in cash. Instead, they stumbled across 3 tonnes of gold bullion. It was Britain's most profitable robbery, a haul that sparked so many spin-off investments over the years that its total worth at today's rates is estimated in the hundreds of millions.

The gang never intended to pull off such a feat. Police had soon made the connection that one of the security guards on duty was a relative of a known criminal. Detectives quickly rounded up the raiders, but not the loot. Most of it had been hidden by fencer Kenneth Noye, who, in turn, needed a man who could turn his red-hot haul into cold hard cash.

As the biggest hunt for stolen property in Metropolitan Police history was launched, Noye asked Palmer's former business partner if he would be interested in doing business. The bullion was ghosted down to the West Country from Essex. Much of it was mixed in with scrap before being melted down in John's smelter and recast. The bars were re-formed into apparently legitimate bullion. Marnie claims that John Palmer had no inkling it was Brink's-Mat loot until it was too late to stop. Like so many of his antics back then, he operated on a 'no questions asked' policy. Such was the gang's audacity – or downright ignorance – that some of the 'new' gold was sold back to the victims of the heist.

A pair of neighbours reported to police that they had seen a crucible operating in Palmer's Georgian home, but when officers visited they said it was outside their jurisdiction to investigate further. It would be another year before Scotland Yard was on the trail. By that point, Marnie and Palmer had jetted off to Tenerife for some winter sun. Police launched an SAS-style dawn swoop on their home, arrested the two unsuspecting house-sitters, and recovered just a solitary gold bar.

Needless to say, John and Marnie were spooked. He was suddenly front-page news, and lying low in Tenerife seemed the best option. Before long, he was named as one of twenty wanted Britons hiding out in Spanish enclaves.

During this extended stay, Palmer set about turning his talents to the rapidly expanding timeshare industry. It would be another eighteen months before Spanish authorities, alerted by their British counterparts, declared him an undesirable alien. He eventually flew to Brazil, but was arrested on the tarmac and forced back to Britain to face the music.

This was just the beginning of a plot that could have been lifted straight from a Hollywood script. Palmer's reputation was largely built on the trial that followed. He was a likeable defendant and argued his case with a smile, saying that while he had certainly melted down plenty of gold as part of his jewellery business, he couldn't possibly know its origins. Police were dumbfounded when the jury believed him.

Everyone now knew him as Goldfinger, yet it was his silver tongue that saved him from the cells. As his Brink's-Mat accomplices were locked up, Marnie watched with shock as John swaggered out of London's Old Bailey and flicked two fingers at the humiliated Scotland Yard detectives in the public gallery.

Palmer was on a roll. His Tenerife holiday business escalated faster than he could ever have hoped. Eventually he was ripping off Britons through a vast timeshare con. He launched a labyrinth of companies to disguise his antics and reportedly relied on the help of a small army of thugs. Police claimed profits were soaring thanks to swindles, violence, racketeering and cash laundering.

At the peak of his offending, Palmer was said to be running a mafia-style firm feared throughout the island. The newspapers claimed his armed heavies launched a swathe of attacks, using knives and baseball bats, across the shady nightspots of Playas de las Americas and the neighbouring resort of Los Cristianos. A Briton was shot dead in a turf war between rival timeshare businesses. If threats or violence from Palmer's henchmen did not work, they could call in two South American heavy-weights, who drove around the resort in a black limousine and were known, by the newspapers at least, as The Sharks.

By the turn of the millennium, Palmer was 105th on *The Sunday Times* Rich List, with an estimated fortune of

£300 million. This Birmingham lad, whose childhood home was so cold the goldfish froze, was now flying around the world on Concorde, with private jets, helicopters and a yacht at his disposal. He got his pilot's licence, bought a French chateau and began collecting classic cars, including a rare 'Gullwing' Mercedes. His yacht, the *Brave Goose of Essex*, was moored in Tenerife's Santa Cruz harbour. He stocked his pond on the island with piranhas and rare albino frogs. Unfortunately for Marnie, he was also investing heavily in two other hobbies: drugs and womanising. Palmer was now openly splitting his time between Marnie and their two daughters, and his mistress, Christina Ketley, who in 1991 bore him a son.

The first cracks in the Palmer empire had already appeared. In 1994, *The Cook Report* television programme secretly recorded Palmer offering to launder up to £60 million a year for an investigator posing as a heroin trafficker. Palmer demanded a 25 per cent commission, saying: 'I'm not cheap, but I'm good.' The Cook dossier was delivered to Scotland Yard, where sources said there was 'cogent intelligence' that Palmer was involved in laundering drug money. But clear evidence also emerged of timeshare fraud. Roy Ramm, a commander in the Metropolitan Police's specialist operations department, said at the time: 'I had to make a decision on what was the best way to spend public money. It's a bit like Al Capone; they got him on tax.'

Then, in 2001, Scotland Yard detectives got the result they had spent years working towards: Palmer behind bars. Police estimated that Palmer had duped at least 17,000 timeshare victims. Investigators untangled a fraudulent network that stretched from dodgy Canary Islands resorts to numbered accounts in countless tax havens.

Palmer accused detectives of waging a vendetta against him because of his acquittal in 1987. Roy Ramm rejected this in the witness box. At least four times during Palmer's questioning of him, Ramm described him as 'a serious organised criminal'. Palmer was eventually given an eight-year jail term – and was later hit with the biggest damages claim in British legal history.

Behind the scenes, as you will read in these pages, Palmer was losing his grip on reality. He admitted to Marnie that he was snorting two grams of cocaine on a modest day. Spiralling further into addiction, his once razor-sharp judgement disintegrated. His decision to represent himself during his fraud trial and his outrageous behaviour in various media interviews illustrate his descent into self-destruction, she believes.

After his release, Marnie felt divorce was all but certain. Christina, a former employee who had received a suspended sentence as a co-conspirator, was now the leading woman in Palmer's life, leaving Marnie saddled with a crumbling mansion and mounting repair bills. She would make three attempts for a decree nisi, but each time John would refuse to sign the papers.

In the decade before his death, Palmer's powers diminished. He returned to Tenerife and found the streets were no longer paved with 24-carat. A friend, Billy Robinson, 58, was ambushed, tortured and murdered along with his wife, Florence, 55, as they drove home from a restaurant to their £1.5 million villa. Mobsters from Eastern Europe were moving in, and violence escalated. Palmer's former head of security, Mohamed Derbah, had struck out in business on his own amid a bitter rift with his former boss. Marnie remembers dining with Derbah regularly. But when Palmer was jailed, Derbah was quoted by one newspaper as saying:'John Palmer is finished on this island. If he comes back and throws his weight around, I have 50 people I can call on to defend my interests.'

Then, on the Easter weekend of 2015, Palmer was linked to Hatton Garden, an extraordinary jewellery heist carried out by at least one known associate, Brian Reader. Rumours swirled in the underworld and the papers that Palmer was in some way connected, even though detectives were sceptical.

Then came his shooting just months later. Palmer was aged 64 and in poor health. Security had been scaled down at the isolated cottage he shared with Christina on the edge of the Weald Country Park, near Brentwood, in Essex. He was also anxious about a host of asset freezing orders and another trial on a long list of charges in Spain relating to alleged timeshare fraud.

Typically for Palmer, even his shooting at point-blank range would raise more questions than answers. After an astonishing oversight by paramedics who declared him dead at the scene, police initially said that his death was not suspicious. Then, six days after the hit, they revealed that a post-mortem examination had shown his body was littered with bullet injuries. Palmer was shot in the right elbow, right breast, right upper abdomen, top of the back, left renal area and left bicep. A ballistics expert would eventually conclude that the gun used was a .32 calibre silenced revolver. Avon and Somerset Police told Marnie investigations by their Essex counterparts were a mess.

So, who did pull the trigger on Goldfinger? 'I'm no angel, but I'm no gangster,' he told one reporter in 1999. 'I've become a silly gangster-legend. They blame me for everything.' It has since emerged that Palmer was under police surveillance at the time of his death, fuelling suspicions he had turned supergrass. Those rumours would have unnerved the criminal fraternity, be they Russian, Spanish or closer to home.

Now, with police nowhere near solving the case, Marnie is finally ready to give her unique insight into Palmer's life, in fascinating and disturbing detail.

In these pages, Marnie relives the extraordinary roller coaster ride – the riches, the glamour and the disastrous denouement.

The life, times and bloody end of the real-life Goldfinger were blockbuster. And Marnie Palmer, his wife of forty years, had the only front-row seat.

Tom Morgan
April 2018

1

KEYSTONE COPS

James could still feel a heartbeat as he desperately begged the 999 operator to help him keep his father alive.

'It's my dad,' he screamed down the phone. 'He's covered in blood. I don't know what's wrong with him … Come on Dad. Please come back.'

No bangs, no voices, not even a dog barking. Nobody heard a peep as John collapsed face down in the turf shortly before 5.30 p.m. on 24 June 2015.

'You're doing everything you can,' the operator told James on his mobile as paramedics and police raced to their country pile near Brentwood, Essex.

John, 64, had undergone gallbladder surgery a week earlier, but had recovered rapidly. He was certainly buoyant enough that afternoon to get under the skin of Christina Ketley, his long-term live-in mistress. After a little tiff, she had driven off at 2 p.m. to go horse riding.

James, in his mid-20s and training for an accountancy qualification, had last seen his dad pottering about in the garden, slurping his coffee and gathering old twigs and branches for the bonfire. It was a typical scene. James then joined his girl-friend for a forty-five-minute workout in the home gym.

By the time they surfaced again from the basement, John was sprawled lifeless on the grass, his pristine white T-shirt – a birthday present from his daughter – drenched in blood.

Detectives reportedly refer to what they call 'the golden hour': the time immediately after the discovery of a body in a murder investigation. It is when they are most likely to find the best clues.

In John's case they didn't just lose an hour, they lost a week. It would be one of the most hopeless starts to a murder investigation in police history.

I'm no expert in detective work and I'm certainly no authority on forensics, but you would imagine any call to HQ that started 'body believed to be John Palmer found at Sandpit Lane, South Weald' would arouse at least a flicker of interest from any officer worth his or her salt. Police had been monitoring the place for more than a decade, and John for thirty years.

Yet the Essex Police officers who eventually arrived on the scene were all too willing to assume there was nothing suspicious about this most notorious criminal dead in a pool of blood. Given a recent keyhole op, they were happy to conclude the wounds had reopened and he'd had a heart attack. The attitude that day was: 'Stick him on the mortuary slab and get the kettle on. Accidental death. Case closed. Home for EastEnders.'

John and I had been married since 1975, but he was now living full-time with Christina and James. Our relationship had deteriorated to the point where I was hopeful of divorce by Christmas.

The news reached me and my older daughter, Janie, in Bath at 6.30 p.m. – an hour after his body was found. I was in the front room of the Coach House watching television when

I heard a roaring engine outside. Through the window I saw Janie's boyfriend, Red, skidding through the front gates in his old rag-top BMW and screeching to a halt sideways.

Red is a reckless fool, but the door slamming and wheel-spins were extreme even for him. He sprinted through Janie's front door and all I could hear suddenly were her screams and howls. Their relationship was always tumultuous, and I initially thought, 'God, what's happened. He's beating her up.'

The phone was ringing from my own kitchen, but I took no notice and sprinted round to see what was going on. All I could hear as I ran up the gravel path were screams of: 'My dad, my dad'. It was terrible.

When I got to her front room window I could see Red chasing after Janie, who had her arms raised and was bellowing: 'Argh, my God, my God.'

My daughter and I weren't speaking. As my divorce loomed, Janie had sworn never to forgive me. I wanted to sell the house I had shared with John for forty years, which would mean she would need to move out of the adjoining cottage. She was in her 30s and I believed she would cope. But John and her boyfriend were telling her she wasn't getting a fair deal.

As I stared through the window, Red came to the door and told me to fuck off. Nothing unusual there – he has always hated me. I went running back to my own kitchen where the phone was still ringing. I picked up the receiver to hear my youngest daughter, Sammy, completely distraught and barely able to speak through her tears.

'It's Dad,' she said, 'He's dead. Please go over to Janie because she will be beside herself.'

Before I had a chance to ask any questions, the line went dead. I sprinted back to Janie's, this time running through her front door, with my arms wide open. I yelled, 'Do you want me?' She raced towards me screaming, 'Mum, mum!' And we put our arms around each other.

Then Red, always thinking of himself, stormed in and shouted, 'You bitch. How can you throw your daughter out of the house?' 'Get out,' Janie said, 'Leave her alone, this is not the time,' and I just said, 'Come to me, whenever you need.'

I wasn't bothered about Red's threats, even when he suggested he would have me 'finished'; it was just the girls and John I needed to worry about at that point. Details of what had actually happened to him were very woolly. Christina had told Red the most likely scenario was a heart attack. I sat on the settee frozen in fear for days as we waited for information. There was nobody we could phone who knew anything. I had never spoken to Christina before, and the emergency services fobbed us off when I tried to ask them for answers.

There were five agonising days before Essex Police showed up. They apologised because they had failed to realise that I was John's widow, his next of kin. Officers had only worked this out thanks to a call from Avon and Somerset Police. The Essex detective sat down out at our kitchen table and told Janie and me that John may have died because of complications after his gallbladder surgery. The medical staff were told of the recent operation when they arrived and had apparently concluded that he had suffered heart failure.

That week was surreal. My daughters were inconsolable, and I was numb. John and I had been through so much. Our marriage was all but over, yet so much was unresolved. I wasn't ready for him to take his secrets to the grave.

I was living in a fog. Then, the following weekend, everything was turned on its head again.

I received a call from a withheld number at noon. It was Christina. For the first time in our lives we exchanged words.

She said: 'Marnie, I'm so sorry about this, but I'm afraid there's some very bad news on its way down there – will you please get Janie home.'

Soon afterwards a police officer arrived. There were strained pleasantries. I asked the young man to get to the point.

'I'm very sorry to tell you that John was murdered,' he said. 'He was shot.'

After several days with their feet up, it seemed that somebody at Essex Police had decided it might be worth chasing up the cause of death. John's body had been left waiting in a hospital morgue over the weekend for a duty pathologist to inspect it. Of course, the post-mortem examination established what had really happened in a matter of seconds.

Further inspection showed John had been shot six times at close range, probably by a professional assassin, using an 8mm .32 calibre pistol fitted with a silencer. The gunman had been hiding behind a 6ft wooden fence, monitoring John's movements through a discreet spy hole that had been drilled into one of the slats. The timing of John's injuries suggested he had been shot soon after getting off his green six-wheel garden buggy.

The jaw-dropping blunders kept coming. Paramedics had warned police at the scene that they had spotted 'small wounds in various stages of coagulation' on John's chest and abdomen. They added that James had said he was unsure if this was connected to the surgery. The two police officers on the scene neglected to examine the body, and failed to call an inspector to the scene or check John's antecedents on the police national computer.

The handsome young detective, with a side-parting and a smart suit, looked like butter wouldn't melt. He relayed all of this to me as he sat at my kitchen table. I couldn't take it in.

This catalogue of mistakes would have made the Keystone Cops blush, and the murder investigation was now a week behind schedule, leaving forensic teams with a near impossible task.

How do you react to that sort of news? In my case, it sparked the biggest breakdown of my life. I suddenly felt so alone in the world. The house where John and I had lived for decades, and where we had brought up our children, was now haunting me. John had turned my two girls against me just months earlier, and now he was dead. I loved him, yet I hated him. I walked out the front door and ran up the long drive towards the busy B-road at rush hour. There was no plan until I started staggering towards the oncoming traffic.

'Kill me, kill me,' I shouted as the headlights bore down on me. I was only wearing a nightdress. No shoes on my feet. The next hour or two is a haze. I remember sitting on a grass verge and being attended to by paramedics. I also recall Janie shout at me to 'pull yourself together'. The police took me to a hospital in Bath and I was assessed for hours.

I returned to the Coach House at 3 a.m., knowing that nothing was ever going to be the same again.

★

John and I were together for four decades and I knew him better than anyone. He came from nothing and was a passionate and loving man. But I had also seen him at his absolute worst. He could be violent, paranoid, ruthless and cruel, as well as being a womaniser and a drug abuser. It was a lifetime of betrayal, and in some ways his death would be a relief.

But in those first few weeks, I was unravelling. I didn't know where the truth began and the lies ended. It may seem strange but within twenty-four hours of finding out that John had been murdered, I vowed to write this book. Somehow, I thought that piecing everything together might help us all understand why John was who he was – and maybe even uncover who killed him.

The chances are you've read the headlines and have already made your mind up about John. I am not here to change that or make excuses for him. Yes, he was violent, ruthless and cruel. The tens of thousands of people he eventually ripped off can vouch for that. But now, perhaps for everyone's sake, it might help to have his true story from the only person who saw it all.

Until now, there were two versions of the John Palmer story. The first version he hated: 'Goldfinger', the most ruthless criminal kingpin of his era – a tale of dirty money, racketeering, violence and intimidation. The second version he revelled in: the working-class lad who became richer than the Queen – the ultimate 1980s 'yuppie' who went from selling scrap to buying Learjets. Both tales were true to a certain extent, but the real story fell somewhere in the middle.

John might have made the same millions had he stayed on the right side of the law. The richest men in the underworld – the really big fish – are not unlike some prominent business executives and world leaders. Greed, lies and ego make the world go round. I can easily imagine John in his favourite pinstripe suit, leaning back in a plush leather chair with his feet on the desk at some investment bank.

But playing by the rules was never even an option for my late husband. He was driven by desperate childhood poverty, and his blood burned to make cash. This ruthless approach bought us a first-class ride around a world that neither of us could even have dreamt of. I just never realised the true price we would all end up paying.

As you will see in these pages, the 1983 Brink's-Mat raid changed everything for John and me. I've heard it said that if you have bought a gold necklace made since then, the chances are that a significant percentage of it comes from that raid, and was melted down in our back garden. I'm not proud of that. Was the heist cursed? Read on, and decide for yourself.

2

HUMBLE BEGINNINGS

'It was so cold at home the goldfish froze one Christmas.'

John loved telling me this anecdote. He wore his childhood hardships in Solihull, Birmingham, like a badge of honour. The pair of us came from deprived homes. Knowing how it feels to be really poor – that genuine fear of going hungry – never leaves you. It drove John to achieve everything he did.

His father, George William Palmer, abandoned his family to shack up with a lover when John was just 5 years old. George ran a shop at one point but never gave his old family a penny. There was no welfare state in those days, no handouts at all. The only breadwinner had fled and the family were on the brink of homelessness. The Palmer siblings had to grow up fast, scratching around to earn every penny, no matter their ages.

John was the youngest of the ragtag bunch. He and his four brothers and two sisters were fiercely loyal to each other and their embattled little mother, Dot. She was tough, but loving. She had her hands full dealing with the most boisterous boys on the block.

Dot spotted something special about John, and always reckoned her youngest son had the luck of the gypsies with him. 'He was born with a lump of lard on his head,' she would say. I had no idea what this meant. She claimed it is a gypsy phrase for those blessed with good fortune.

'It's from his father,' she would say. 'He is from French traveller stock. Somehow he will always find a way to come up on top.'

George, the eldest brother, was straight-laced, as were his sisters. The other brothers, however, were like peas in a pod – sticking together and constantly getting into scrapes.

David and Mike both struggled with mental health. Dave was a loose cannon, probably the naughtiest. He would show up in the middle of the night in stolen cars. It was always a drama. He would hammer the horn and flash his headlights towards our bedroom window until John let him in and gave him a feed. David was eventually caught at an airport with a huge stash of drugs. He died of a heart attack while locked up for drug trafficking in a prison on the Isle of Wight.

Mike was also a handful, owing to his schizophrenia. For years it went undiagnosed, but John always looked after him. During his episodes, he battered his girlfriend, and even tried to burn down Dot's house at one point. Like David, he died young and in tragic circumstances.

The fourth brother, Midge, was most like John. Both of them had good business brains, were willing to cut a few corners, and had God-given gifts for charming even the most miserly customer. The pair could and would work in synch with each other when it came to making money.

The boys stuck together like glue because they had to. Not a week went by without a scrap kicking off in the street. John might have had a fearsome reputation later in life but the Palmers weren't even the most formidable family on their own street.

Their working-class district had a fierce gang culture, stretching back decades before John. I smiled when I saw the drama *Peaky Blinders* on television. The gangs were much scruffier by the time John arrived but that ruthless lifestyle was still thriving.

The family never had enough money to heat their home, but Dot instilled in them the golden rule: Never show weakness.

John went to school on and off until he was 13. He put bags on his feet because his plimsolls had holes in them and, for years, he would wet himself in class. In private, his brothers would give him hell about his little pee problem, but nobody else would have dared bully him about it. His older brothers always looked out for him, even if it meant chaperoning him home when his trousers were sodden. Midge would escort him without fail when he had one of his accidents.

The Palmer household was a place where you always needed to be on your toes. The brothers would roar with laughter together, and get up to all sorts of mischief. Home life was raucous, and there were occasional brushes with the law: usually petty thefts or street fights. Without a father around, they had grown up angry.

It is all too easy to judge, but the brothers were doing everything they could to bring money in. They begged, borrowed and took any work they could get. Mike had regular work on the roofs, and would often bung John a tenner for help humping tiles around. John also helped Midge out on the markets.

John was an entrepreneur from the very start. With no qualifications, he had to be. By 14, he was going house to house like a rag and bone man asking if anyone had anything they wanted to sell. He had such a sharp eye for a bargain and was soon making more cash than everyone but Midge.

John and Midge were a great team. Throughout their teens they bounced between jobs in Birmingham. The two of them were blessed with silver tongues and an appetite for hard graft. For both the brothers, deal-making was instinctive.

Midge had a big market stall. He worked seven days a week shifting anything he could get his hands on. Bedding, towels, clocks, you name it. He did really well and was a huge influence on John.

Work with either Midge or Mike was regular but John had bigger ambitions. At 17, he travelled down to Bristol with Mike, who had a girlfriend in the city. Something clicked in John: he loved the place. A weekend stay with Mike turned into a couple of weeks before they both moved down permanently.

Despite knowing barely a soul in the city, John and Mike were soon making ends meet by selling leather belts in pubs and at markets. They would get the leather from a Bristol tannery and make these things themselves. Neither of them had a clue about fashion but John had such an uncanny ability to find a gap in the market. Doing his rounds of the pubs, he quickly made friends and always ended a conversation by asking: 'Anything you're looking to sell?'

★

My own childhood had been lonely, and we were pretty hard up as well. My mother, Jean, couldn't even afford to run a bath for me; we had a tin one that we shared with the neighbour next door. Their child, Squeaks, would have the first wash, then me. We were so short of cash that all my long hair was cut off once to sell to wigmakers.

I loved my father but unfortunately I saw him getting up to no good – he had his fancy women on the side. One of them, a barmaid, gave me a toy spinning set. Despite hating that young woman for stealing my dad, I cherished that spinning set for years.

My mother was a telephonist who was once the voice of the talking clock. She also boasted of being a 'bluebell girl' synchronised swimmer in Brighton and claimed she swam the English Channel. I always found this story hard to believe as she was quite overweight when I grew up. In fact, I was always worried about getting fat like her. People would compare me to Brigitte Bardot. It was flattering, but made me very self-conscious. I was determined not to put on a pound of weight, and I starved myself on cheese crackers for most of my teens. These days you would probably say I had an eating disorder.

As a young child, everything I did annoyed my mother. She seemed to resent me however I behaved. For one reason or another, she just never seemed to want me around. I had no siblings and I think my birth must have been a mistake as far as she was concerned.

She abandoned me for several years after I turned 7. I remember it like it was yesterday. She ran off with a new man, and left me home alone in our worker's cottage in Totnes, Devon. I hung on to her legs begging her not to go. I can still taste the tears running down my face.

The door slammed shut and I was left to fend for myself. Eventually, my Nan was called over. She told me I had been alone in the cottage for three days and that she would take me to her home to start afresh.

All I took with me was my teddy, which I dragged everywhere. It had a long red ribbon that would trail along the ground and forever trip people up. The thing must have been filthy. I do remember a friend of mine, Susan, stuffed the bear up her living room chimney once. Bear was never the same again.

My years with my Nan saved me. I was very close with her. She and my granddad had opened a fishmonger and a florist after moving to Totnes from Sussex. Both of them were outgoing characters and had very lively outlooks for their generation. My Nan was very proud that she was the first lady driver in Brighton. She loved cars and so did I. She also told me my grandfather was in the *Guinness Book of Records* for catching the biggest trout and salmon in Devon.

My granddad wasn't in good shape by the time I was born. He had come home from the war with a shrapnel wound, and died in hospital when I was small. But as a keen fisherwoman myself, I was always very impressed by his trout exploits. Still to this day, I boast about him!

Having been abandoned by my mum, I was quite clingy around Nan, and would try to go out with her whenever I could. She often cooked tripe and onions. You could smell it wherever you went – disgusting. But I would have eaten it morning, noon and night if it meant I could stay with her.

I was a generally poorly child, possibly owing to a bout of TB that went undiagnosed. Doctors found scarring on my lungs when I was 8. I also spent weeks in hospital after badly breaking my arm when I was 9. The milkman had picked me up and swung me around, but then lost his grip. They kept me in hospital for weeks but my mother never came to visit me. In those days, parents didn't show their children as much affection as they do now, but I never got over it.

In the months afterwards, I was a real handful for Nan. I lived with her for another five years, but she hated me carousing and I had got to an age where I started to take an interest in boys. By the time I was 14 she told me she couldn't cope.

She said: 'Your mother doesn't want you, your father doesn't want you – what am I to do?'

In the end, though, she did hand me back to my mum. My mother and now stepfather were living in a flat in the inner city suburb of St Paul's, Bristol.

My mum came to pick me up soon after my Nan moved to Paignton. By 14, I thought I was a mini-adult. I was waiting tables in cafes in Devon and doing a paper round. But I was in for a real eye-opener about life in the city when I arrived in Bristol. St Paul's had a heavy influx of immigrants at the time, and was a flashpoint for racial tension. Drugs and prostitution were very blatant on the streets. I was a naive young girl from the sticks, but from that point on I grew up very quickly. Mum made it clear I would need to earn my keep, so I searched for work and never went back to school.

I really wanted to work with horses, but my Nan had always told me there was no money in it. Instead, I decided I would be a good hairdresser, and got a Saturday job at a salon on Gloucester Road. To my delight, they offered me an apprenticeship. My mum agreed to front up my indenture for 100 guineas. It was my big break. They agreed to pay me 10s a week for three years.

A year or so into my training, my mum and stepdad got a house in Filton, north Bristol. It was a much longer trip to work and my salary was so low, it would cost me half my pay packet to get there on the bus. I remember asking my mum for a loan to pay my bus fare.

'Walk there and back,' she snapped back. 'It will toughen you up. This is the real world.'

As a teen, I knew she was threatened by me. Her looks had faded and men were starting to pay attention to me. She even hated the fact that I got on with her new husband. I vowed to move out as soon as I could afford it, but, as it turned out, I had to flee with barely a penny to my name after my mother falsely accused me of stealing a brooch. As punishment, she shut me in my bedroom for two days with no food or water. I was barely 16 but I knew I was not welcome. I would need to my find my own bedsit.

I didn't know all that many people, and I wanted to stay out of the way, so I would go out on my own at night and meet people. Within months, I met a good-looking young chap called Finbar Ryan. He was a 19-year-old jobless drifter and, to be honest, I fell for him simply because he was so good-looking. Then he asked me to marry him after just a few weeks.

Despite my brief rift with mum, I got in touch with my stepdad to see what he thought of Finbar's proposal. He said I should wait for someone with more ambition in life, but I took no notice. I was a child. I didn't have a clue, but I saw it as a way to get a foothold in adult life. We were wed at a Catholic church when I was 18 and found a bedsit in Redland, a nice area of Bristol.

Predictably, within a few months, the young marriage fell apart. Finbar was a nice enough bloke but he had absolutely no pride or get-up-and-go. I loved my cars and clothes, but he couldn't care less about making his name or even earning a few possessions. We didn't even have a TV. After six months of nagging him to get a job, I walked out on him and back home to my mum and stepdad. They had spotted it before me: I wanted more in life.

A couple of months later I managed to afford a little shared council flat in Barton Hill, a down-at-the-heel area of the city. It was very basic, but I was so proud to be on my own two feet. I loved the hairdressing and moved to a more upmarket salon at Westbury, then one on Corn Street, and eventually Headz on Whiteladies Road, where I rented a chair and recruited another young girl called Diana to help me out. Diana and I became inseparable. We still see each other today.

It had been a relatively amicable split with Finbar but I was in no rush to meet someone, especially as I waited for my divorce to go through. A couple of men asked me out, including a lovely man called Paul, who would regularly take me away for the weekend. We used to go to Bath or Torquay.

I coloured my hair from brunette to blonde and, by the age of 20, I was fully independent and a fully qualified hairdresser. I was having a lovely time of it.

★

John and I clapped eyes on each other for the first time in a seedy old nightclub on Park Street, just off Bristol's city centre, in the winter of 1972. I was aged 24, John 22.

I was actually on a date with another chap, David, who was DJing. He invited me along at 9.30 p.m. for a drink together before the crowds arrived. Having shown up on time, I can remember speaking to him for ten minutes before he started his music set. I was at a loose end, just hanging around watching him play, and must have looked very bored as I leant against the bar, with my chin resting on my palm.

As the club steadily filled with people from the neighbouring pubs, a swarthy young man tapped me on the shoulder. 'I'm John. Can I get you a drink?'

I immediately noticed the squeaky Midlands accent, and how good-looking he was. Dark twinkling eyes, slim build. Brooding and handsome, but scruffy.

'You need a haircut,' I told him. 'Come to my salon on Whiteladies Road. I'll sort it out.'

He probably thought I was flirting, but I wasn't. I was keen to drum up any business I could get. After a couple of minutes of pleasantries, my drink arrived so I turned on my heel and headed to the dancefloor alone.

I don't think I gave him a second thought until a few hours later. David the DJ and I were about to leave when I noticed John stretched out asleep on a settee in the club. He looked like a tramp, and I was taken aback when David wandered over to him and woke him up. The pair of them knew each other. They had a laugh and we all walked out together at 1 a.m. as they whispered in each other's ears.

David and I got in his Ford Anglia, and we waved our good-byes as John crossed the road and got in his gold Jaguar E-type. I have always loved my cars, and the E-type is just the most beautiful of all. I do remember thinking to myself: 'I hope I see that John again. If only so I can sit in that car.'

After leaving the club, I went back with David to his house on the Wells Road, in Knowle. Aside from the car, John hadn't made a great impression on me. He was good-looking, but a bit shorter than most of the men I would have gone for in those days. I could tell I was a couple of years older than him, too.

Then, a few days later, John turned up at my salon asking for the haircut I had offered. He was with his brother, Midge, and I could sense within a matter of seconds that John looked up to him. There was a real camaraderie between them. That day, though, John only had eyes for me. I was flattered by the attention.

Over the next couple of weeks, I carried on seeing the DJ, just for something to do in the evenings. He liked taking me along to his parties, just as a bit of arm candy. It was obvious neither of us was really that bothered about the other but

I enjoyed getting out of the flat and meeting his friends, especially John, who always had a story to tell when he would show up for a late-night drink at the Birdcage, a nice little upmarket bar in Clifton.

I always had a rush of excitement when we bumped into him, even though he was so badly dressed – often in tracksuit bottoms and scuffed trainers.

John had that monotone Midlands accent, which made him seem immediately down to earth. But I could tell he was also very streetwise and sharp. He had a twinkle in his eye, and was confident in an understated way. John was barely in his 20s, but he had the posture and presence of a man fifteen years his senior. However, it would be two months before romance sparked.

A girlfriend of mine had an old yellow Triumph Spitfire and I would often pester her about having a go behind the wheel. Eventually she agreed to let me take it for a quick spin around the Clifton Triangle. With a grin as wide as the River Avon, I remember flooring this little sports car up Park Street.

Unfortunately, as I turned around the corner, I drove straight into the back of a parked taxi. It was an almighty bump and I sat behind the wheel in tears as the taxi driver jumped out of his car, screaming every expletive known to man. But then amid the huge kerfuffle, a calm voice came from behind me: 'Don't you worry about a thing, Marnie – I'll sort this out.'

It was John. He had watched the whole thing from across the road. I was so relieved to see him. He had a look at the front of the car. It was all but a write-off.

'I'll get two pals to pick up the car,' he said. 'And I'll take you home.'

This was John's knight in shining armour act. When we got home we slept with each other for the first time, and that was that – he had me.

3

FAMILY FIRST

If you walk around Bristol these days, you will see expensive coffee shops, smart office workers and trendy haircuts; in the 1970s it was very different. The mixture of maritime history and an influx of immigrants meant there were always business opportunities for a wheeler-dealer like John. He felt at home among the more edgy characters, where deals were brokered with no questions asked.

After our night of passion together, I agreed to start dating John. I was wide-eyed and blonde, he was dark and swarthy. I wasn't keen on moving too quickly, but we would go out a couple of times a week.

John was never a massive drinker, but he enjoyed the nightlife in Bristol. He liked a gamble, and enjoyed ducking and diving around some of the less salubrious drinking dens the city had to offer. It was on a night out in a smoky West Indian bar in St Paul's that he met another ambitious young chap called Jonny Groves. They got on very well and Jonny soon suggested John could join his round selling Calor Gas. To John's glee, Jonny said, 'We'll split profits 50/50.'

Of course, John jumped at the chance. The business did pretty well and it wasn't long before he and Jonny were in enough profit to rent a cheap plot of land selling barely roadworthy old bangers.

Arthur Daley would have been proud of some of the wrecks John sold on City Road, St Paul's. The area, in those days, was rife with vice: prostitution and drugs. John wasn't into that but he was streetwise. There was no income tax and certainly no guarantees for customers at his fledgling car garage. It's fair to say he had a few disappointed punters, but John didn't care. He wanted to make a name for himself in Bristol by making money as quickly as possible. He would try his hand at anything to do so.

Our first weekend away was a trip to a market in Stratford-upon-Avon. This was my first insight into the way John's business brain worked. Midge was running a stall selling china, rugs and housewares. They set me up as a fake customer. My job was to pretend I was buying all their gear to attract other punters: 'Ooh, what a bargain.'

You'd imagine people would get wise to it, but the ruse worked a treat. The customers flocked around as they watched me fill my bags. I really enjoyed being a part of it. The banter between John and his siblings was uplifting to be around. At the end of the day, Midge gave me £5 for my help. We were giggling that whole weekend. The next day, I remember we visited John's uncle and aunt to see their pigs. John absolutely loved pigs; he was adorable. To look at his silly little smiling face, you would never have believed the newspaper stories that would one day be written about him.

We stayed with John's mum at the two up, two down where they had all grown up. Wallpaper was hanging off the wall and the place was filthy. Three of the siblings still had to share beds.

The morning we left, John was sat at the kitchen table and started breaking wind to the tune of a nursery rhyme – Baa Baa Black Sheep, I think. I was dumbstruck with horror, but they all fell about laughing.

I didn't admire the squalor or their choice of jokes at breakfast, but I did envy the camaraderie of their family. That warmth was never present in my own childhood home.

★

Back home in Bristol, John was keen to impress on me that he was a man who was going places. But his smooth-talking spiel often came unstuck with hilarious consequences.

One night he took me to a nightclub in the upmarket Whiteladies Road area near my salon. As we walked in, the music came to a sudden halt and the packed room fell silent. As everyone looked around, the DJ pointed at us and screamed: 'Oi, you! Come here!'

As we walked over, he shouted: 'That car you sold me. The engine dropped out as I went over a hump bridge. It's a complete wreck.'

The bloke made a right scene and even John looked embarrassed. We left the club with our heads bowed and had a drink at a nearby hotel.

'You should be more careful,' I said. 'You can't get away with ripping people off like that. It's a small city.'

But John laughed back at me: 'That bloke in the club was one of the lucky ones. Another punter bought a car with no engine at all.'

'That's awful,' I said, failing to see the funny side. Little did I know then that I would soon be falling foul of one of his dodgy motors.

Despite wowing me on our first encounter with his E-type, John wasn't quite as rich as the image suggested. In fact, he had picked up that car on the cheap. There would be a string of other giveaways, too. In our very early days he gave me the keys to a very old Ford Anglia from his forecourt. He thought it would make it easier to meet up for dates. He was being flash. On my first journey, I had to do a three-point turn to park. As I tried to put it in reverse, the gear stick came out in my hand. I didn't know what to do. I was left just stuck there, blocking both directions of a residential street in Clifton. I got out, grabbed my bag, and walked down the road to work.

In another bid to impress me, John said he had a flat for me in the city centre. I was amazed until I saw it. It was so bleak, and it looked like a filthy drugs den, without a bed or any furniture. I tried to convince myself I could do up the place. A bit of elbow grease never killed anyone. But I soon gave up. There was no power, and when I turned on the tap in the kitchen, dust, instead of water, came flooding out.

There were plenty of these misfiring romantic gestures in the early days. Our first Christmas together was disastrous. He asked me what I wanted and I said a John Lennon LP. Instead, he bought me a Paul McCartney one. To make matters worse he wrote 'Mirium' on my card and gave me a size 14 dress from Dorothy Perkins. I was a size 8, on a diet of just cola, crackers and Philadelphia cheese. I cried and had a little tantrum when I first saw it all, but then we fell about laughing.

On my next birthday, he asked me again: 'What do you want Marnie? I'll get it right this time!'

I showed him a Timex watch in the Dingles catalogue.

'You've seen it, John,' I told him. 'It's the same as the one I bought for my mum.'

Did he get it? Not a chance. He presented me with an old lady's-style watch. That was the last time he was doing the shopping for anything. But you couldn't fault John for trying. He wanted me to be like a princess, even though he was yet to have the riches to match his intentions.

The reality was that I was easily impressed by flashiness back then and, admittedly, I was a bit of a diva. I was doing a bit of modelling as well as hairdressing. I was keen to make some money, too. My own childhood had made me acutely aware of what I wanted and how little I would be prepared to compromise.

I supported John's huge ambitions. I knew he had the drive, charm and savvy to make a success of himself. The change in his lifestyle, and mine, for that matter, would be rapid as he worked his socks off to build a name in the sales trade. When we met he was living in a shared house on a shabby old mattress on the floor. Yet within a few months he had wads of cash to splash out on holidays and cars. It was all show, but sometimes in life that works. John was so determined, he was like a man possessed.

The banger car business was doing well. Never complain, never explain, was the business motto. He was also picking up other bits of scrap to sell on. Soon, he was renting a car forecourt in Clifton, the poshest area of the city.

We went for regular meals out like most couples would. John would get recognised in certain places because he was such a wheeler-dealer. He was the sort of bloke who would know everyone in the bar by the end of the night. Sundays were the best nights out with John. We often went to the same Italian. John would always order spaghetti bolognese or the T-bone steak.

John was a night owl. Four or five evenings a week were spent meeting mates, making business deals and having a gamble along the way. He told me they would always go to the casino into the early hours and then have breakfast together.

The early days were very passionate, with lots of sex. But we would often squabble too, and there was an early warning sign of violence. Once, as he came at me screaming, I hit him over the head with a saucepan. He erupted with rage and slapped me around the chops.

John would often pester me for threesomes, too. I thought he was joking, but it all came to a head during one heavy night out on a weekend in Torquay, Devon. We were meeting his brothers, Midge and David, and their partners. John was really showing off over dinner and then we went back to a friend's place for a drink. The men kept disappearing off to the loos and coming back even noisier and in fits of giggles. To my horror, John started kissing David's wife. Then this friend of John started trying to kiss me.

I pushed him away and screamed. Midge found it all hilarious, but I got up and ran out to the street. I was beside myself. Eventually a police officer found me and I explained what had happened. The officer took me back to the house. John hit the roof after that, and told me they had been taking drugs.

'You idiot. Why did you take a police officer here – he could have arrested the lot of us!'

I was furious with him for having a go at me. I had no idea they were all nipping out to smoke pot.

The violence and now this sordid little incident. I told him I'd had enough. We didn't speak for weeks, and I even started seeing Paul again.

I think we were apart for two months. John repeatedly begged me to come back, and one night he followed me out. I was walking with Paul to the Mandrake club in the city centre. We hadn't even stepped inside when John kicked off.

He sprinted over and hit poor Paul in the face. That poor bloke got a horrible kicking because of me and I swore I wouldn't go near John again.

It was around that time that a former fiancée of John showed up at Headz. She warned me that John had beaten up a friend of hers, too. I figured he must have been unravelling.

'You're welcome to him,' I told this girl. 'Not interested.'

I ignored his calls for months but he wasn't one to give up. John turned up on my doorstep one weekday afternoon. He stood there in the pouring rain, in the doorway, with a suitcase and a Harlequin Great Dane puppy.

'Can I stay with you for a bit Marnie,' he said. 'I'm finding us the most wonderful place to live. You are the one.'

I had previously seen a Great Dane on a trip to Norwich with my ex-husband, and my heart had been set on owning one. I remembered I had mentioned this to John. Seeing him with that dog just melted me on the spot. I still found something in John so endearing, despite all the warning signs.

John said he was sorry for everything, and that he wanted me to be his wife. He just couldn't cope with the thought of being without me. Reluctantly, I agreed to let him stay a couple of nights at the Whiteladies Road flat.

We named the Great Dane Quincy, and she would come everywhere with us. We took her to Cheddar on one of our first dates since being reunited. She would even join us at the Caravan Club nightspot in Bristol, and even at dinner with my mum and stepdad. We were a very funny little collection. She was almost as big as me, but wouldn't have hurt a fly. We later bought a young male puppy, Jerry, for her to have a mate.

We would go up to Solihull quite regularly in those days to see John's mother and brothers. Quincy joined us on a rowing boat trip in Saltford, near Bath, on the way home. She was so heavy and cumbersome that we nearly capsized.

After being reunited, John seemed to go into overdrive to impress me. I think it had been a shock to him to see how easily I could move on and he couldn't. It definitely bucked his ideas up to see that other men were interested in me, and that I was perfectly happy to spend time with my own friends if he wasn't around.

I told him I was worried about money. He seemed to be spending so much, and we were getting behind on the household bills. He put his arm around me and said: 'Don't you worry about it. I will always look after you, whatever happens.'

All the bills were paid the next day. John, it seemed, had learned his lesson and was starting to behave. The businesses were all making good money, and he was treating me very well. He was hungry to make a name for himself, but also the happiest I can remember him. We had some lovely little holidays; one to the Old Bank Hotel, in Jersey. John said he would buy a place there one day.

He would take me out a lot and shower me with gifts. In those days the casinos were a huge part of his life. I didn't have a clue what I was doing on the tables, but he would always give me between £5 and £20 to fritter away. Men at that time used to say I looked like a film star. I took that with a large pinch of salt, but I must say I did feel like I'd walked off the silver screen as I gambled away John's cash with a glass of champagne in hand.

With all the late hours he was keeping, I did become eager to keep an eye on him so I trained to become a croupier. I lasted about three weeks. The hours and the maths made my brain fizz. I preferred hairdressing.

Trying my luck, I cheekily told him I wanted a Rolex watch. He came back to the flat with a Cartier. I threw it back to him, just to tease him. But he wasn't amused. The very next day he drove to a dealer in Somerset and bought a real Rolex. It was the first one I had ever seen. By that point, he had won me over.

As well as dogs and watches, John indulged me in my greatest passion of all: cars. My Nan and I were the biggest car nuts. You didn't get many women in my day who knew all the makes and models, but I was obsessed. Porsche was always my favourite. I dreamed of having a 911 from the day they came out in 1963. John told me he would get me a Porsche one day, but for now at least he would get me an MG Midget, which I loved. It was teal blue with coffee leather seats. It was on hire purchase but we could easily afford it.

He always made sure I was in the nicest cars. He later sold the MG and let me have his E-type. It was stunning. So fast, and probably the most beautiful car on the road. I would love seeing the boy racers at the lights. They would always look at me thinking I was a soft touch, but their smirks soon slipped as I floored it away. It was beautiful, and extraordinary to think just months earlier we had been sleeping on the floor on an old mattress.

By the summer of 1973 we had moved into a nice one-bedroom basement flat in Redland. It seemed so luxurious compared to the squalor of the bedsits and houses we had both been sharing. We had the old dark silver Rolls-Royce and E-type parked outside. I thought we were the business.

Then, just a few months later, I got home to find a note saying he had got us a bungalow, in Whitchurch, and for me to come there to the address. It was such a lovely little house with a garden. We quickly agreed to move in.

Giving people the impression of wealth – however fleeting – gave us both a buzz. John loved jumping in the Rolls-Royce for a meal out with my parents. My mum and stepdad were bowled over by this posh new man in my life as we arrived outside their house with curtains twitching on their road in Henleaze.

The illusion was shattered on the return journey, however, when John ran out of petrol in Patchway, a rundown district of north Bristol. My stepdad had to get out and help push this great hulk of a vehicle up a hill to the nearest garage. The poor old chap was huffing, puffing and wheezing with every step. Typical John, I thought. Grand ideas, delivered with the panache of Frank Spencer.

My stepdad was worn out that night, but, fortunately, amused. I think he found it endearing. John had worked his magic on him, he was everything my ex-husband wasn't. My dad knew John had fire and ambition in his belly, and it would take a bloke like that to keep me in check.

With my parents' approval, he asked me to marry him. In typical John fashion, the proposal was less than romantic.

'I've been getting these headaches,' he said, after getting on one knee. 'The doctor said the only way I would get rid of them would be to settle down and get wed.'

Yet again I didn't know whether to laugh or cry. I've heard of men getting married because they were getting earache – but headaches? That was a new one!

Amazingly, it wasn't a joke. Dr McCarthy had told John it would make him feel more confident, secure and relaxed.

'I've been burned already,' I told John. 'My last marriage didn't last – if I do it again, it has to be forever.'

He nodded in agreement.

'And I won't be having children,' I insisted. 'My own childhood was unhappy. I'm not interested in all that.'

There was a fly in the ointment: I was still technically married to Finbar. John was very practical about it all though, and once we got hold of my ex-husband, the divorce quickly went through.

John was also happy for me to put career before family in those days. He was the driving force behind setting up my own salon. He was so encouraging.

'You can do it, Marnie,' he would say. 'Working for yourself is the best thing for you. Who needs a boss ordering you around and taking your money?'

It had never even occurred to me to go it alone. I asked Diana if she was keen to go into business with me, and with John's help, we took the plunge. We found a little basement shop at 10 George Street in Bath. It was a wreck inside but John could turn his hand to anything. With the help of Diana's husband Mark, they renovated the whole place in weeks. It would be the start of some very happy years for me. It was lovely to be out on my own, making my own money.

I came up with the name Areba because it sounded a little bit like my favourite shop in the world, Biba, in Kensington, West London. Diana and I used to go up to visit this amazing place every month. It was wonderful – these were the days of Roxy Music, and the decor and clothes were all black and gold. It was the bee's knees, and I wanted my salon to be the same.

One time John had driven me up to Biba for inspiration. We parked just around the corner, but when we returned the car was nowhere to be seen. John was going nuts, convinced it had been pinched. Eventually we phoned the police but nothing had been reported. Hours later we discovered it had been towed as it was illegally parked. My trips to Biba weren't quite so regular after that!

In early 1974, we moved to a rented house in Pendennis Road, Staple Hill. I couldn't believe we could afford this big, wonderful place, with sprawling grounds stretching three-quarters of an acre. The council let us rent it on a temporary basis, as it was due to be torn down. To celebrate our luxurious new place, John bought me my first horse. I remember feeling like a princess as we took the Rolls to the National Trust's Dyrham Park, a spectacular seventeenth-century mansion, to look at Polly, a gorgeous white mare. We bought her and Katie, another mare, for £1,000. John even gave me another £600 for a saddle.

Initially, I kept Polly in a field in Winterbourne, but she was far too used to more luxurious surroundings, so I persuaded John to let me keep her at Dyrham Park stables again. John and I loved riding at Dyrham, and he was as besotted as me. He was a natural with the horses, and he had an instinctive gift for riding. He could tame even the most difficult animal. He had no fear.

I was so excited to be marrying a man going places, but I didn't keep my engagement ring long. That winter we were broken into. We had both come home from work at the same time to find all the doors open. My engagement ring had been stolen and, perhaps most upsetting of all, the tropical fish were dead because the power had been pulled out of the heater for the tank. We had a black pony who was very spooked by the episode and, when the police came over the next day, it bit one of the officers on the bottom. I really didn't know whether to laugh or cry.

We were married at Bristol Register Office on 24 September 1975. Conscious that I had already been wed, it was a low-key affair – just our parents and a couple of friends. We had a laugh by making our Great Danes, Quincy and Jerry, the guests of honour. I invited the *Bath Evening Chronicle* for a bit of publicity for the salon. It made a huge splash on page one the following day. The dogs looked brilliant with us in our 1970s get-up in those pictures. The caption was 'Bath hairdresser gets wed'. That would be the first, last and only time that it was me rather than John, but I was quite proud of my bit of PR.

'It's not just John who has the business brain,' I thought to myself.

They were such happy times but I always sensed something was missing for John. I could see how happy he was around Midge's kids. Despite my own feelings about motherhood, I knew John was a family man a heart. He always looked after his old mother, and would eventually buy her two houses. He also did everything he could for two of his more troubled brothers. When I asked him if he wanted me to come off the pill, he was delighted. I was pregnant within weeks. There was no turning back now.

This wasn't long after we had converted Areba, and the business was still finding its feet. My mum told me I was making the biggest mistake of my life.

'Get rid of it,' she said. 'What will you do with the child when you're working? It can't come to the salon. You can't keep it in that dingy basement. It's got to go. You'd be mad to keep it.'

We took no notice; my mum could be very bitter. I knew how much John wanted the child, and I had come around to the idea, too. Then, to top it all off, Quincy got pregnant, too.

Before I had my first daughter, we had one last holiday to the Seychelles. John was at his happiest there. It was the most wonderful place, our first taste of holidaying with the elite. I got food poisoning one night and John went out alone and met Jon Pertwee, the actor who played Doctor Who and

Worzel Gummidge. He said Pertwee was a charming chap; I was miffed that I had missed him.

Homelife at Pendennis Road was such a happy time for John. He seemed so content, and, initially at least, he was very attentive around me.

My first daughter, Janie, was born on 6 September 1977, at Southmead Hospital. It was a very difficult birth and John stayed with me throughout. The doctors eventually had to take me into theatre and use forceps. When she was born, seeing her in John's arms made my heart sing.

John had wanted a dynasty for himself but, when we got back to Pendennis Road, he made it clear he wouldn't always be a hands-on dad. He was a good dad to Janie but it was a very busy time for him. His mother, Dot, came down to help me and it was nice to have her around.

The baby wasn't the only new arrival in the Palmer household. Quincy had her seven puppies just a few days after Janie was born. In the garden we also had Polly and Kate, the two horses; Alfred, a black ram; Blacky, a grumpy pony; five kittens, and a jackdaw. It was chaos.

John was particularly fond of 'Jack' the jackdaw. He had climbed out on the chimney at Pendennis Road to pinch him from his nest as a chick. He then trained the bird to follow him everywhere. That bird was a right nuisance, always flapping around my head wherever I went. I remember one December he kept swooping down to pinch food as I made the Christmas pudding. Jack eventually died after falling in some wallpaper paste. We were decorating the spare room for Janie and went downstairs for a cup of tea. When we returned we just saw him head down in all that sticky goo.

In later years, when we moved home, John found and trained more jackdaw chicks, and we also started a menagerie.

He was forever bringing new birds back, sometimes with horrific consequences. He put a tawny owl he had found in the cage with the cockatiels one night. The next morning it was like a murder scene – blood everywhere. All that was left was the owl and a dozen cockatiel heads scattered on the ground.

I shared John's interest in ornithology. I went on a bird of prey course and bought two Harris's hawks. They really made me realise how lucky I was, being able to train them to hunt around our estate. They would catch all sorts – usually pheasants and rabbits. I occasionally hunted with them when I was on horseback; one arm outstretched for them to land on my gloved hand. They were so majestic. It was the most amazing, magical feeling watching those huge birds in action. They lived with us for years, in the aviary, but I initially bonded them together in the house – tethered of course, and a safe distance from the cats. Amazingly, in later years, they never bothered the other pets when flying free. It was incredible how clever they were.

My closest friends at the time were Diana, who I worked with, and Pam, who I got to know while cutting her hair. Both of them were very independent-minded and outgoing. It was a real tonic to meet young ladies who were up for making the most out of life.

Pam was a British Airways airhostess and she was married to Dave, a former pilot who, we were told, lost his licence after crashing drunk into an aircraft hangar. John got on very well with Dave. The pair of them took us to a friend of theirs in Cardiff for a lovely meal one weekend. Our host told us she made fur coats, and John agreed to buy one for £1,800 as a present for me. It was the most beautiful white fur, and became my pride and joy.

I think John's money impressed Dave, and a few weeks later he asked for a big loan to set up business. John turned him down as he was an ex-bankrupt. John often said he felt guilty about saying no, but it was the wrong time for him. Had Dave asked years later, John would have handed him a blank cheque.

4

METEORIC RISE

John was well on his way to his first million by the time he was 25. People will say he cheated his way to the top, but I saw how hard he grafted to get there.

After coming home from a long day's work, John would sit down at the kitchen table and regularly pull out a rolled up wad of notes from his bag. He was in love with cash. Often, with a wry smile, he would hold his earnings up to his face and breathe it in. 'I love the way it smells,' he would say.

Even at this stage, he didn't trust the banks to look after his beloved notes. By the time we moved to our long-term family home in 1981, he kept wads of cash all over our property instead of sticking it in his account. I would come across money hidden in socks in the wardrobe, under the bed, and even stuffed underneath our fitted drawers in the kitchen. The really valuable stuff would eventually be kept in a secret vault built into the cobbles in our stables.

His biggest early break was getting to know Garth Chappell. The pair of them had hit it off after meeting in a pub. They both had a network of contacts across the city, and

Garth persuaded John there was money to be made in the carpets business.

The pair of them launched Bristol Flooring at 144 Bedminster Road, south of the river that runs through Bristol. Having honed his salesman skills working on the markets of Solihull, shifting carpets in Bristol was child's play for John. That sparkle in his eye, confidence and easy charm had punters eating out of his hand. It was a completely legitimate enterprise; John and Garth were able to cut out competition by buying a small range of carpets wholesale and selling them cheaper than anyone else in Bristol. There was a real boom in home improvements in those days, and customers couldn't get enough of their stock.

At work, my husband was full of energy and exuberance – the buzz from making good money was coursing through his veins. Garth was very similar. They were kindred spirits, revelling in their jobs, having both known hardship as children.

The pair of them had insatiable work ethics. When they weren't shifting carpets, they were in their van touring the West Country picking up old scrap to sell on. They bought a gold and silver campervan with blacked out windows. It was filled every day with stock to sell at fairs, markets and the high street. The pair were always looking for a new angle to make a profit; one person's junk was often another person's antique.

John was working all hours. He was completely addicted to the hustle, and I would have to settle for being second best. Right from the very start of our relationship he had made this clear to me. When we first got a flat together, sometimes he would pop in just for an hour, wolf his dinner down, place a £5 note on the dinner table, and then head out for the evening again.

Now, Janie was around, but work still came first. I needed to show John my career was also a priority, so I went back to the salon as soon as I could. Long maternity leave wasn't such a thing in those days; I wanted to be back making money.

Each morning we would jump in the cars at the same time and head in opposite directions down Pendennis Road; John to Bristol, and me to the Bath salon. I would take baby Janie in and all the clients would make such a fuss of her. She had a cot beside the hairdressing chair, and she would normally sleep right through. Even so, I did cut down my hours. The only day I worked a full eight hours was Saturday. It was my slice of real life.

I enjoyed the two salaries coming in, especially as every new venture seemed even more successful for John and Garth. The scrap business soon outpaced the carpets – their gear was moving so quickly, John soon had enough to get leases on a couple of shops.

Garth and John started advertising for 'unwanted scrap' in the papers, and set up a limited firm called Scadlynn. The take-up was huge and the phone never stopped ringing. These were the last days of the rag and bone man – families were used to offloading their unwanted stuff to a man with a horse and cart. But as those businesses dried up, there was a vacuum in the market. Garth and John exploited the opportunity. Forget Steptoe and Son; there was a new band in town.

The one hiccup for John was that suddenly there were so many cheques to write. He was buying in a heck of a lot of gear but he hated getting the chequebook out. It wasn't that he didn't want to pay; it was his fear of writing anything that crippled him. Writing his own name was a challenge for John, let alone spelling anyone else's. He found it very embarrassing. Regularly he would get me to fill them out for him in advance, so he could simply write in the numbers when he picked up the stock.

Throughout this time, he was, by and large, keeping his nose clean. Police were aware of his dealings, but would have considered him no more seriously than a Del Boy-style character; always ducking and diving, but doing nobody much harm.

We had been married about four years when we moved into Garth's old home at 10 The Park, Willsbridge, between Bristol and Bath, in 1979. Joan, Garth's wife, had lovely taste and it was another huge step up the ladder for us. The house had a fabulous garden, with enough room for the horses and our donkey.

Garth and Joan had moved on to a lovely house with a pool in Dundry. Ever the competitors, we were a bit envious when we saw it. However, we loved our home at Willsbridge.

At the end of the garden, John had set up his workshop. He was out there one afternoon when he came up with an idea that changed the rest of his life: he decided to build an industrial-scale smelter. He hit upon the idea because of the vast quantities of old gold that were being sold as scrap. All those unwanted gold teeth could become hugely desirable gold rings, he thought.

The smelter was made of huge bricks and corrugated iron. It took just a couple of days to build and was tucked in behind a stable, in a lean-to. John never saw any need to hide it. On the contrary, he was proud of the smelter. He enjoyed showing anyone and everyone.

It was very much trial and error at first, but John soon got the hang of burning all the metal down and recasting it into new shapes. The heat that thing gave off was incredible; it could have kept our whole home warm.

John was amazed to find hardly anyone around Bristol had access to a smelter. The techniques he used were hardly new; they've been around since the Stone Age. Copper, silver, gold, lead and tin were the first materials to be melted down thousands of years ago as they have comparatively low melting points.

In the first few weeks, that crucible was fired up night after night and I worried about all the smoke. We would have plumes of black soot in the air, and it was especially awkward on a Sunday morning. I'm sure the neighbours hated it, but John just rolled his eyes at me: 'This will change everything for the business. You'll be glad when the money starts coming in.'

He was right. The smelter was an instant money-making machine. In the early days we were there, I was pestering John non-stop about paying the domestic bills. Within a few months of the new business venture, any money worries vanished. In fact, by the end of the 1979–80 financial year, Scadlynn Ltd had a turnover of £4 million.

I think John was pretty addicted to it. You see men crowding round the barbecue or bonfire, and this was no different. He was like a caveman, mesmerised by the roaring flames. Unwanted cast-offs from dealers, merchants and car boot sales were transformed into desirable, sought-after jewellery. John's knack for turning people's rubbish into profit was amazing. Gold and silver was so popular then, and the best stuff was recast and sold in our shops in Bath and Cardiff. The rest could be shifted at the markets.

Garth and John agreed they would make far more money if they abandoned the carpet business altogether and concentrated on shifting all the gold they were getting on their scrap rounds. That decision was another masterstroke. Scadlynn remained above the old carpet shop on 84 Bedminster Road, but Bristol Flooring was sold off to two brothers. With the proceeds, John invested a couple of thousand pounds in marketing. A huge newspaper advert campaign across the region read: 'We will pay top £ for your unwanted jewellery'.

The return was ridiculous; so much came in that it was almost overwhelming. John and Garth ran out of room in the Bedminster depot so bagfuls were coming back to The Park. We had to find a way of sorting it quickly before selling it on. The smelter was brilliant for melting everything down, and then John would recast it all as desirable jewellery. It was the perfect solution.

John became utterly obsessed with the smelter, and making as much money as he could as quickly as possible. This was the early 1980s and Thatcher was slashing taxes, encouraging everyone to make it on their own. Life was being very good to John.

There were many country shows back then across Somerset, Gloucestershire, Wiltshire and beyond. John and Garth would take the campervan with its suspension buckling under the weight of all the gear they had to sell. Often they would come home having sold the lot, and the van would be full of new gear to melt down. They made it look easy.

Business was booming as nobody in the entire south of England was smelting down old jewellery on the same scale. Soon, rather than traipsing around the country in a van, his network of contacts began delivering jewellery and scrap to our home. They hired a team to help smelt it all.

In those early days, my mum, Nan and I had a small but crucial role in sorting all the scrap for the smelter. It became a family ritual waiting for John to come back armed with plastic bags crammed full of unwanted jewellery.

My mum and Nan were absolutely fascinated. John brought home sacks full of gold teeth, old cutlery, all sorts. We were like magpies swooping in on silver milk bottle tops. Some of the jewellery that people got rid of was stunning.

The sacks weighed such a lot and we would empty them out in my daughter Janie's old plastic bath from Mothercare. This bath, with duck motifs on the side, took centre stage in the living room for hours on end. Other girls my age might be out carousing and dancing, but this, as far as I was concerned, beat a disco hands down.

I got such a buzz searching and picking out the most glittering, eye-catching jewellery. My mother and my Nan enjoyed it as much as me. The three of us would have a right giggle trying on some of the old castoffs, deciding which bits to keep. After being sorted in the bath, the majority of unwanted scrap was handed back to John, who would drag it all down to the garden and then fire up the smelter the following morning. You would then see the smoke coming out of the chimney for days.

With work so busy, John and Garth sold off the Bedminster carpet shop and all their other business interests: Scadlynn was more than enough to keep them going.

Garth was content, but John had his eye on the next prize. The business partners decided Garth should take sole control of day-to-day activities while John would pursue his own project: three upmarket jewellers, one in Bath, one in Bristol and one in Cardiff. Suddenly my scruffy husband was in an expensive suit. He started dealing on a large scale with London's Hatton Garden, the capital of Britain's jewellery trade.

The London connection came with inevitable pressures. Garth was usually the go-between with the slippery city types who were sending vans full of jewellery to melt down. But John was happy with the extra business that came in. It felt like there was a bottomless pit of money for everyone involved.

For John, paperwork was a bore, and so was sticking by the rules. There was a run-in with police for obtaining credit on furniture by providing false references, and in the summer of 1980 the pair of them appeared in court facing charges. John insisted to me it sounded much worse that it really was. He said they had just provided a couple of false signatures as they were in a rush. It was a really silly thing to have done, and John received a six-month suspended prison sentence.

I was annoyed with John, but he didn't care about the conviction. He was making too much money to worry – so long as he wasn't behind bars. He and Garth were always willing to cut a few corners, but nobody who knew them then would have described them as villains. Anyone from their background would do the same.

Despite the conviction, John was hardly an enemy of the state. In fact, between 1979 and 1983, one of our most regular visitors was a local bobby. The friendly officer, always with a smile on his face, loved popping in for a weekly cuppa while out on his rounds. Over the months he became very good mates with John. This officer would stand there chatting – sometimes while still on shift – as John poured all the unwanted jewellery, gold teeth, broken candlesticks, whatever, into the smelter.

The officer knew John's business inside-out. A few years later, he felt he had no choice but to declare his friendship with us and resign from Avon and Somerset Police. I still feel sad for him that he felt that was necessary.

Scadlynn's profits had given John and Garth a national profile and it wasn't long before the Hatton Garden jewellers twigged that we had a money-making machine in our back garden. The markets and shops in the West Country were good money, but the sales potential in London was on a different scale.

As time wore on, John increasingly focused on the shops and Garth was in charge of the day-to-day running at

Scadlynn as well as dealings with the big city types. Gold values were soaring and we were able to trade with jewellers in the capital's West End. Now they were dealing with the big boys. Less than a decade on from living in abject poverty, John was a rich man.

We made enough money to buy a sparkling white Mercedes convertible, another E-type Jaguar, and also plan another move up the housing ladder. John said he had found a place called the Coach House near Bath that I might like. When I arrived for the viewing I went weak at the knees. I couldn't believe my eyes. It was a wonderful Georgian pile at Battlefields near Lansdown, built by the noted Bath architect John Wood the Younger. Standing in its historic hallway, we both fell in love with it.

'Surely we can't afford it,' I thought. I felt like Eliza Doolittle in *My Fair Lady*.

We sold 10 The Park pretty quickly and then shook hands on a deal for the Coach House. We took out a huge mortgage but it was the most unbelievable bargain. We were besotted with the place. It would be my home for the next thirty-four years.

We had so much room; it was like nowhere I had been before, let alone lived in. Initially the purchase only included the Coach House and a 1-acre plot. But, over the years, we bought Chapel Cottage, a charming little property just 10ft away from our sidewall, on an endowment mortgage, and then, three years later again, the surrounding meadows and woodland. The whole estate would eventually be 33 acres, including eight stables with tack and feed rooms, an Olympic-sized training area and a labyrinth of outbuildings. There was also a summer house, outdoor swimming pool, landscaped gardens, woodlands and a lake.

The place was my paradise. The kitchen and drawing room had views to the rear garden and front courtyard. The views of the surrounding countryside were wonderful, and I had all the space I would need to look after my horses. I adored the grounds, which included an enchanting private walled garden, a small pond and an orchard. The place was so tranquil, and just fifteen minutes' drive from the salon.

The property also adjoined the monument for the Battle of Lansdowne fought in 1643 in the surrounding valley. Apparently the Cavaliers and the Roundheads went to war across our land in the battle for control of England. The place had amazing history, and it still seems perverse that, for our generation at least, the property would attract more attention because of John's ugly-looking smelter!

John loved that home as much as I did, and he soon put his own eccentric stamp on it. He would race around the grounds on four-wheel drive buggies and scramblers, and every week he seemed to turn up with weird and wonderful new purchases to furnish our opulent estate. Some of the additions you might expect of a respectable jewellery and bullion dealer: oil paintings, Chinese vases, carriage clocks and classic cars. But the other stuff he brought back was downright weird: pot-bellied pigs, a menagerie of birds, a gypsy caravan, an old tractor, and a lamb.

In the first decade after we bought the house in 1981, there were many renovations, rebuilds and extensions – mostly, in our ignorance, before we received planning permission. Initially, John built a guest flat on the property and improved the stables. It was all 'build it now, get the paperwork done later'.

I ended up having an equestrian facility to rival an Olympic athlete's. We also had a wonderful converted barn that stored John's amazing collection of cars. I'll have to draw breath before I list them. Eventually they included a V12 Mercedes, an 'O' reg

Jaguar, an old Rolls-Royce, two 1960s Ferraris, a classic tractor, a John Player Special black and gold Minivan, a Mini Cooper, a Sierra Cosworth, and even a rare Maserati, bought from John's car dealer pal John Dangerfield. The one that got away was an Aston Martin Vantage – he had one on order for months, but police investigations put paid to that dream.

John recognised he needed to start looking the part. The scruffy look would have to go, he agreed, but he didn't have the time and patience to get a suit fitted. Instead, I wandered into the most expensive suit shop in Bath and tried to pick some for him.

The assistant at Christopher Barry, a renowned tailor with a shop in the city centre, looked confused as I explained: 'My husband needs a good suit, but he won't be coming in. He hates clothes shopping.'

However, perhaps realising we had a decent budget, he agreed to come over to our home to meet John for a fitting. We bought four designer suits at a couple of thousand each and a dozen shirts and ties so we wouldn't have to go back for some time.

He looked mouth-watering to me in this smart get-up. After a lifetime in scruffy work clothes, I think it gave him a real taste for fine tailoring. John remained obsessed with moving on to even bigger and better things. We had a millionaires' playground and John was by that time a jewellery trader of repute across the region. Now he looked the part, too.

'You can sell snow to the Eskimos in that,' I told him.

However, I would soon realise that the smelter in the back garden was more alluring to investors than any Savile Row suit.

Initially, John put the furnace in with my horses in the stables at our new home but I wasn't happy about this as there was so much smoke. My two horses might as well have been sleeping in a sauna. I was convinced it would kill the animals, so I eventually convinced John to move it further down the field. This was no huge problem for him – he had a couple of burly assistants to help him. John and his pals put the smelter in a corrugated iron shed at the opposite corner of our grounds from the stables. It was also now a reassuring distance from the house, a one minute walk from the back door down to a stone arch that had been in the grounds for hundreds of years. The smelter was built right next to it, in full view of passers-by. We certainly weren't trying to hide it.

For me, it was out of sight, out of mind. I had a little toddler to look after and was soon expecting a second daughter. The smelter was becoming very sought after as John and Garth's reputation in the business continued to spread across London.

Little surprise, then, that Britain's underworld would see his metal-melting enterprise as a potential dream ticket. For the men behind the Brink's-Mat raid, that smelter was a gilt-edged gift from the gods.

5

FOOLS' GOLD

The Brink's-Mat gold was just too hot to handle; even John would come to rue the day it landed on our doorstep.

The robbery would eventually be a half a billion pound bonanza for the underworld, yet it left a thirty-year trail of blood and ruined dozens of lives. 'Fools' Gold' was how it came to be bitterly referred to by associates of those involved. I, for one, can vouch for that description.

As we snored in our beds in blissful ignorance, our fate was sealed by dawn on 26 November 1983. Micky McAvoy, who wore a yellow balaclava topped off with a trilby hat, and his gang had swooped at a warehouse at Heathrow shortly after 6.40 a.m. They doused the guards with kerosene and threatened to set them alight unless they opened the vaults. Once inside, they found 6,800 little gold bars – all the same size as Mars bars.

On the face of it, the raiders were criminal geniuses. The reality was not so impressive. The gang had no idea they would stumble across the gold. Instead, their inside man Anthony Black, the brother-in-law of gang member Brian 'The Colonel'

Robinson, had told them to expect £3 million in cash. To make matters worse, Black had opened the door of the warehouse ten minutes late, having slept in. The whole robbery took two hours, when it should have taken twenty minutes.

The loot they were targeting was a ridiculous underestimate, yet, without a thought for the consequences, the gang took the lot. It weighed down their van and they had to drive slowly out of Heathrow, the heavy vehicle scraping on its tyres.

It was the biggest story in town at the time. I remember John and I waking up with the rest of Britain to hear it breaking as the top story on the radio news.

Instead of laying low after the robbery, the raiders splashed cash on property in Kent and Essex like it was going out of fashion. There was even one story suggesting McAvoy had bought two Rottweiler dogs to protect his new home and named them Brinks and Mat.

Detectives quickly made the family connection between Black and Robinson, and the following February Black, nicknamed the 'Golden Mole' by the tabloids, was sentenced to six years at the Old Bailey.

Anyone with half a brain would have told them that stealing the gold would be the easy bit. Making the loot vanish and turn to cash would be the true conjuring trick.

It would be months before John got involved. The robbers had turned to crime boss Kenneth Noye, and his right-hand man Brian Reader, to fence the loot. It was then, via their Hatton Garden contacts, that our little business in the West Country was identified. Noye and Reader knew the gold ingots had to be melted down to get rid of their traceable serial numbers, and that selling pure unidentified gold would be too suspicious. Only a completely different grade of bullion would put investigators off the trace.

Scadlynn Ltd was their first port of call. The middlemen told Garth they had come into some scrap gold to melt down. They watched as Garth showed his contacts how he and John had been maximising profits by mixing with scrap, copper and other metals.

'Bingo,' thought Noye.

Noye started off sending a few ingots, before steadily increasing the amounts over a matter of weeks. Soon it was coming down the M4 thick and fast. Reader was also at one point said to have taken briefcases full of gold bars on the train from London to Bedminster, in Bristol.

It may sound naive, but I genuinely believe John and Garth didn't initially realise they were handling Brink's-Mat gold. I'm not saying for one minute that the boys were squeaky clean, but their business was always dependent on a little bit of discretion. There's far too much bravado in that world and, by the time they twigged, it was too late to pull out.

The ingots were beautiful; they glistened and were perfectly formed. I saw about ten bars at the Coach House, but genuinely thought nothing of it as we were getting bagfuls of valuable jewellery coming in every day. Like everything else, the gold was just shoved in with all the scrap – unwanted rings, broken gold teeth or damaged necklaces.

John was busier than normal over those few weeks, but not enough to make me suspicious. With the jewellers doing well, that smelter was a hobby rather than our main source of income. Over a few weeks, however, I did notice he was dashing out there as soon as he got in. Sometimes he would pop out before he had even removed his tie.

Garth was bringing the bullion to the Coach House because they had too much to get through at Scadlynn's office, where there was another smelter. Over a matter of weeks, the drop-offs became so regular that John lost his rag with Garth. He called him on the phone in the kitchen.

'It's too fucking much, Garth,' he said. 'Much too much.'

John would be dubbed a 'mastermind' for turning the red-hot ingots into cold hard cash. But, as I saw with my own eyes, this was not rocket science. He just carried on doing what he always had done – mixing everything together with the unwanted jewellery. John was worried about what he and Garth had got themselves into, but he never mentioned this to me. By that stage, there was no turning back.

After the gold left our property, I really have no idea where it went. As much as 70 per cent of the haul has never been traced and is said to be still sloshing around London's criminal underworld and property market today. Some of it was allegedly smuggled in Tupperware boxes to Britain from Holland, where it had been taken after the raid as part of a complex additional 'earner' involving the VAT, but I honestly couldn't see John getting involved in that. He could barely sign his own cheques. Other large sums were supposedly invested in the Docklands boom of the 1980s and '90s. There were even reports that a portion was used to buy a section of Cheltenham Ladies' College, which was then converted and sold off into flats.

But back in 1984, Brink's-Mat could not have been further from our minds. John was focused on making the jewellery businesses work; he had left Garth in sole charge of Scadlynn. John was doing the odd bit of smelting work at home for him, but the major ambition for him now was to become a jewellery dealer of national repute.

I was also completely preoccupied, as I was pregnant with my second daughter, Sammy.

When she was born, there was a real change in John. I felt very isolated. Having been so good in hospital for the birth of

Janie, he was suddenly cold and sullen. He wasn't there for the birth and he barely even spoke to us when he picked us up from hospital to take us home. I was sat on the back seat. He fixed a stare on me in the rear-view mirror. 'You won't stop me from working,' he said.

I was gobsmacked by his cold demeanour. He dropped me off at home, and then disappeared until the evening. I was shattered. That same day he brought his mother, Dot, down from Birmingham to help me. As soon as she arrived, John placed little Sammy in her grandmother's arms and took me out to the stables. He pointed around at the horses and our amazing equestrian centre.

'This is what you do. This is your job. Do not ever interfere in my work or ever try to stop me working. It's none of your business.

'Go back inside, look after our children and look after our horses. The rest you can leave to me. I'm going back to work.'

I went back into the Coach House crying. I had only given birth a few days before. I was absolutely devastated; I couldn't understand why he was being so brutal.

John stayed outside until 3 a.m. He went down to his hunting lodge and fired up a barbecue to share with his friends.

Fortunately for me, John's mum had seen all this, and was very cross with John.

'You should know better, son,' she screamed at him.

After hearing about everything she had been through with his father, I knew exactly what was going through her head and why she was so angry. I was pleasantly surprised she hadn't taken his side on it. Instead, she really got on his back. It was such a relief, as she was the only person on the planet who could tell John what to do. She stayed for weeks and really put John in his place. 'Family comes first,' she would tell him.

Years later, she died of a blood clot just hours after being rushed into hospital with leg pains. When she was gone, there really was no talking sense into John.

Fresh from his telling off from his mum, I went to work repairing our relationship. I told John we were going on holiday. In October 1984 I booked us a trip to Tenerife via the package travel agent Lunn Poly. I still have the receipt. I was so excited.

The trip was our fifth to the island in just a few years. I used to book trips all the time, and John didn't mind – he just paid. We loved the winter sun. It was a recommendation of Diana's. We were doing really well financially, but we weren't quite in the Barbados ranks yet, so the Canary Islands were perfect. We might have thought twice had we known Kate Adie, the BBC reporter, and pretty much every hack on Fleet Street would be joining us around the swimming pool!

Before we flew out, my only worry was that John's family passport was about to run out. All of us were named on it, as that was how it worked in those days. I nagged John about getting it renewed countless times in the weeks before. There was no way he suspected he was destined to become a fugitive. Had he thought he was in trouble, John would definitely have made sure he had the right travel documents. In fact, he seemed very relaxed about the trip. The newspapers would later print that we flew to Spain to flee arrest, but that was complete nonsense.

We flew out in January 1985 on a two-week package deal. We had £1,000 in cash, two suitcases, and our two young girls, Janie, then 7, and Sammy, still a baby. I can just recall us sitting back and looking at the drinks menu as we took our seats on the plane.

'Business is good,' he said, ordering a brandy. 'We deserve a break.'

Most of the more wealthy Spaniards travelled to the north of the island in the Santa Cruz area, but we found a place we liked on Playas de las Americas, near Los Cristianos. In those days it was completely different. The ruling family had left that part with their youngest son and much of the sand was considered a wasteland. Las Americas was just a road with a couple of rundown hotels and some down-at-heel Moroccan shops.

The hotel we were staying at offered horseback riding. I was always keen and John fancied it, too. We went for miles on a pair of young Arabian horses and ended up off road towards the sea.

The horses were skittish and extremely difficult to ride. The paths we took were also terrible, littered with huge rocks and potholes. My knuckles were aching with the strain as I tried to stay balanced, but John wanted to keep riding. He loved showing off. Everyone could see how well he could ride, even on tricky terrain. It was an adventure.

We were galloping for a mile or two and then, all of a sudden, we came to a long isolated beach, and were surrounded by derelict building sites. You could see work there had been abandoned fairly recently, but grass was growing on the foundations, and some of the wood was rotting away.

When we got back, John asked the rep and then the hotel staff about the derelict sites.

'It is very sad, Mr Palmer. A Spanish businessman wanted to start a timeshare business but his wife left him and he went bankrupt. The project was going well until the money ran out.'

John asked what a timeshare was. He had never even heard of the phrase. 'It is when you lease an apartment between several different holiday homeowners,' said the member of staff.

John thought it was incredible idea. He was always open-minded about potential new business deals, and he loved

Tenerife. We had stayed in different hotels on our four previous trips to the island, and been to Playas de las Americas at least three times. We knew it could be a success.

John really fancied a slice of this. At the time it just seemed like dreamy summer holiday talk; it was typical 'I could live here' chat as we lazed around on the sun-loungers. But this time John meant it, and it was the start of the biggest business venture of his life.

We did our research on the timeshare idea. A German entrepreneur, Alexander Nette, had made plenty of money in the late 1960s after coming up with the idea. Its original appeal was to offer consumers an affordable compromise between booking a holiday in the same resort each year and owning a holiday home outright. At the time, Spain was the most popular country for timeshare resorts, with more than 35 per cent of all European timeshares located there.

The Spanish had then turned their attention to the Canaries and started building several potential timeshare plots in the area, but there had been rows over money with locals. John saw this as an opportunity. The locals might prefer to deal with his money than the imperialist Spanish. I preferred Spain or Lanzarote, but he was convinced there was more potential here.

We got back to our hotel that afternoon full of optimism. We were staying at the Hotel Troya, on Playas de las Americas. The surrounding resort wasn't anything like it is today, but the hotel itself was pretty luxurious. The sun was shining in January and the girls were having a lovely time paddling in the pool.

Unfortunately, our holiday bliss wouldn't last long. A few days later a call came through on the hotel intercom for us to report to reception. The staff said that I needed to call my mum urgently. The receptionist then guided me to the phone booth. I dialled home and my stepdad answered after barely half a ring.

'Your house, your house,' said my stepdad, breathlessly. 'It's the SAS, they've raided your house.'

I couldn't believe what I was hearing. It made no sense. I screamed across the atrium at John to get on the phone.

'It's the police,' my stepdad told John. 'They're at your home looking for the Brink's-Mat gold. It's all over the television and the reporters are saying police want to arrest you.'

John was shocked. The blood seemed to drain from his face, and he was shaking.

'Don't worry love,' he said. I was thinking: 'Don't worry? Our world is falling apart!'

Unbeknown to John, he and Garth had been under surveillance for months; police had been waiting for the right moment to pounce. You might have thought they would have noticed we were out of the country.

Coordinated raids were rushed forward when, fourteen months after the robbery, an undercover team was exposed in the grounds of Kenneth Noye's country mansion in West Kingsdown, Kent.

Noye, the suspected 'top fence', was alerted by his guard dogs barking at shadows in the corner of his garden at night. He then discovered one of the detectives, John Fordham, lurking between trees. Before Fordham had a chance to say who he was, Noye stabbed him to death.

The detective's partner called for urgent back-up and a huge police operation swung into action ahead of schedule. Noye was arrested and eleven of the gold bars – the only original ones found at the time – were discovered in his 18-acre grounds. They were wrapped in red-and-white cloth hidden in a shallow gully beside the garage wall.

With their surveillance operation in chaos, officers had to act on all their intelligence immediately. Our home at the Coach House, Garth's house, and Scadlynn in Bedminster were next in their sights.

Back home, our good friends John and Carol Thomas were housesitting. They were such a kind couple and Carol was great with the horses. The pair of them had the shock of their lives when the police swooped at 6 a.m.

Police swarmed our huge estate, thinking there might be some sort of shootout. Officers came smashing through the front and back doors in unison. Carol sprinted upstairs in terror, assuming they were being raided by a violent gang. She was preparing to jump 14ft on to the roof of the stables when the police burst in and pinned her to the ground. She would have broken her legs had she not been stopped by officers, who wrongly mistook her for me and arrested her. Carol's husband, John, was also arrested at the property. How the police could have mistaken him for my John I will never know. They look absolutely nothing alike; my John wasn't blond for a start.

Both John and Carol explained who they were and that we were in Tenerife, but the police wouldn't believe their story – they were both taken away and questioned until the next day at Bridewell station, in central Bristol.

'We know absolutely nothing,' Carol told the police. 'You can interview us until Christmas if you like. This is as much a waste of your time as it is ours.'

Thelma, a sweet old lady who lived next door, was also in for a nasty turn. About an hour later there was a tap on her back door. This was a regular morning ritual for Thelma as our ducks would waddle round to pester her for bread. She assumed the tapping was the birds as normal. However, as she appeared bleary-eyed in the doorway, she was confronted by two men in their SAS-style get-up. She immediately burst into tears.

The incompetence of the police still amazes me. We had flown out on holiday three days before they had swooped. They must have known that. The heavy-handed treatment of Carol and John was completely unnecessary.

The police drilled holes in the floor and walls looking for the bullion, but only recovered one bit of gold, left underneath a cushion on the settee. They also seized what they claimed was a key piece of evidence: Noye's phone number written on a phone book. To this day, I believe this was planted. It would be a helpful part of John's defence when handwriting experts concluded the scrawl did not match either John's or my handwriting style.

The police took everything they could; even our brand new Range Rover Vogue, which had arrived just a few weeks earlier. However, despite the painstaking searches, I was delighted that they failed to find our safe underneath the cobbles. I don't think there was any Brink's-Mat gold in there, but they did miss a good deal of our precious jewellery. John thought the sniffer dogs failed to catch the scent because there was so much horse hay and manure in the stables.

Needless to say, I was white with shock at news of the raid. But John stayed pretty calm. He took a few minutes to take it all in, sitting down at his table in the corner of our hotel room. Then, the first thing he did was get on the phone to his brother, Midge. It was a race against time to get some of the stock away from the sticky fingers of the police. John had a lot of mates who had been in trouble. We knew they would try to freeze his assets and accounts.

'Get rid of everything,' John told Midge. 'The police want to take me to the cleaners.'

Within a few hours, journalists and photographers started turning up at the hotel. First, it was just one or two. By the end of week there must have been twenty. It was mayhem. To my surprise, John decided very early on that he would talk to the media. 'I've nothing to hide,' he would tell them all.

In many ways the dialogue with them was useful. Journalists told us the raid was part of coordinated swoops across the UK, and that police had already picked up Noye and Garth.

This worried John. He knew there was a multi-million-pound police investigation ongoing, bigger than any in Scotland Yard's history. Police had formed a forty-five-member task force to delve into money laundering and organised crime. The gold robbery had become its main assignment. For seven months, the team visited banking centres around the world, and determined that some proceeds of the gold robbery were tied up in shell companies that laundered profits from drugs and other illegal activities. John got on the phone to a solicitor. He was worried about Garth, and fuming also that we were being linked with Noye.

Garth was quickly charged with handling the bullion. Detectives also pulled in Terry Patch, who had done bits of donkey work at Scadlynn. Initially, John wanted to convince police that he would cooperate. But the longer it went on, the less John wanted to go back and face the music. We were front page news and it was scary.

'They're going for the jugular, Marnie,' John told me. 'I need time to work out what to do. Midge will need to help us.'

John and Carol were such a great help. They kindly returned to the Coach House after the raid, and said they would stay on for as long as we needed. It must have been a huge hassle, with journalists, photographers and even police keeping a close watch.

My John was furious that he was in the frame but he put on a very brave, calm face and faced a dozen or so TV and newspaper interviews. He was determined to win the PR war, and I think part of him relished the attention. He told reporters that he found it bemusing that the police were making us out to be geniuses.

We were anything but, he proclaimed, telling one reporter: 'The situation was ridiculous. My passport was about to expire. If we had any plans to stage a runaway, we might have thought about getting the travel documents sorted.'

John agreed to do almost every interview he was offered. He repeatedly called the raid 'Mat-Brink's' rather than Brink's-Mat, and claimed to know nothing about it.

Police were still searching our home when John's interview with Kate Adie was the lead on the night's BBC news. More than eight million people tuned in to see John and me, poolside. It was mind-boggling.

'John Palmer is a jeweller and bullion dealer,' Adie said in the broadcast. 'With his name very much in the news, his home raided by police, its grounds searched, and several of his friends and colleagues being questioned, it might have been thought that he would have wanted to go to ground in Tenerife. Not at all.'

Against the backdrop of our hotel, she added: 'Amongst all the holidaymakers, he was to be found with his family and some friends intent on pursuing his holiday, and giving his views on the past few days.'

The TV footage then cut to John, who said: 'I feel that the police have overreacted. I think they have got carried away. I understand they carried out SAS-type raids at my property. I think this was unnecessary. There were some simple, honest people looking after my property and I think they've [the police] completely overreacted. I'm just amazed at it.'

Adie added: 'The police have been looking at a small smelting works which are in the grounds of your house.'

John responded: 'We have in the grounds of our house a smelter which was put there approximately three years ago. These works were connected with my former business, which was a bullion company.'

Adie said: 'So you do claim to be completely innocent?'

John said: 'I am completely innocent of anything to do with this so-called Mat-Brink [sic] bullion raid. I know nothing of it and nobody I'm connected with knows anything about it either.'

The interview riled Scotland Yard. It looked so shabby on their part, John hammering them on primetime TV. Police confirmed to the BBC that they couldn't go out and arrest John, but officers had alerted Interpol to monitor airports.

John didn't consider himself a villain; it wasn't all an act for the likes of Adie and the press. But the media scrutiny was so intense and we were quickly coming to the conclusion that they were not willing to believe our side of the story.

It was such a confusing time. We were holed up in this hotel with nowhere to go and no idea what to do. The extradition situation was very complicated, but there was no European Arrest Warrant then so British authorities were, for the time being, powerless to get Spain to cooperate.

'Going home at this stage isn't an option, I need to take care of business before the police tear us apart,' John told me just a day or two before we were due to fly back.

The following day, as our package deal came to an end, John agreed to a final interview.

Adie introduced her piece: 'After three weeks in the sun the tourists left their package trip from Tenerife to Bristol this morning – but without John Palmer and his family.

'When he first he heard he was wanted by the Met Police, he sat on in the sun and insisted he would finish his holiday, even though his house had been thoroughly searched in his absence, and a former colleague Garth Chappell was arrested and charged.

'Yesterday he hinted he might not be going home immediately. Here he explains why he might not go home to face the music.'

John said: 'The first two weeks were ruined by the press, and we just plan to take another couple of weeks now … Whatever's going to happen to me in Britain will happen in two weeks' time as well as it would today. I've had some contact with a member of the C11 at Scotland Yard.'

When Adie asked if he thought he had anything to fear, John snapped back: 'No, I'm completely innocent, I've got nothing to fear.'

As far as I'm aware, the Met Police never tried to contact us while we were still in Tenerife. But John, via the media, hoped he had sent them his clear message: 'I am an innocent man, and I will stay here while my name is cleared.'

John knew by this stage that he had been under investigation for months. Several weeks before we flew out, police had told John there had been a threat on his life. An officer had turned up on our doorstep out of the blue. We thought it was weird at the time. Now we wondered if that visit had been a ruse to allow them into our property so they could bug our calls. A couple of officers had entered the property, and it all seemed rather odd. Nobody we knew at that time would have wanted him dead.

That night John's old pal Jonny Groves flew out and helped smuggle us all out of the hotel and into their holiday apartment while we worked out what we were going to do. We left the hotel at 2 a.m. and paid the bill. I was convinced the media were going to spot us as I had a crying baby with me. Janie, then aged 7, was also with us.

We were now overnight exiles. Thankfully people on the island were very kind to us. We would be introduced to a British expat called Terry McKay, and he told us he loved living on the island. Terry had his villa in a complex, and was travelling backwards and forwards to London all the time. He had a lovely quality of life.

'I love it out here,' Terry told us. 'Sun all year, and there are so many ways to make a few quid.'

Our relationship with Terry became a huge help, and we hid at his place for weeks. It had a pool, and staying there kept us sane while we were under the most intense pressure.

It was troubling when we heard reports from home that Noye had stabbed a detective involved in the case. John and Noye had never been in the same room as each other before we flew out to Tenerife – they had no idea who each other was. A lot has been written about John having a close association with Noye, but I know that's not true. Garth had been the go-between.

A steady flow of money arrived for us as friends flew out to check on us. The wads of cash were sent by Midge, who was busy selling all the jewellery from the shops to ensure we could extend our stay indefinitely. Midge and his wife, Karen, were brilliant. As the weeks rolled on, we would even end up getting Midge to sell our cars for cash. I told John to sell whatever he needed apart from my beloved Nan's jewellery. Unfortunately, by mistake, even that was auctioned off. It was very upsetting.

As if he didn't already have enough worries, John was also very concerned about his other brother, Mike. He felt guilty that he wasn't around to keep an eye on him. Mike's behaviour was erratic, weird, and he had been forever turning up unannounced. John gave him money, whatever he needed, but Mike was becoming a lost soul.

Mike was diagnosed with schizophrenia but repeatedly abandoned his medication. Eventually, we heard he had attempted to knife his partner, Sadie, and had been sectioned. I was terrified about him coming round again but John never gave up on him. He was then in and out of institutions for years before eventually moving back up to their mother's home. Unfortunately, he was again abusive and even tried to burn down the family house. He ended up dying in hospital after a string of relapses. John was like a stone about most emotions, but he was very protective of his brother. Mike's situation really upset him.

6

NEW LIFE

Tenerife was always the biggest and best-known of all the Canary Islands. However, as John launched his empire there, its tourism industry was still finding its feet. A horrific plane crash in 1977 hadn't helped; two jumbo jets collided on the Tenerife North Airport runway, killing 583 people. The setback sent prices tumbling on tourism developments as holidaymakers opted for perceived 'safer bets' on the Spanish Costas. The island is less than 200 miles from the African coast, making it a neat stop-off point for imports to Europe. For some – including me – the grey volcanic beaches were far from enticing. But, for John, low land prices presented an opportunity. Tenerife had one trump card on the rest of Europe – all-year-round sun. The prospect of a 365-day a year tourism scheme was mouth-watering. Despite my preference for Spain, or even Lanzarote, John was right to want a slice.

The raid and subsequent fugitive status over Brink's-Mat left John with a lot of time on his hands, but there was no point getting bogged down worrying. Being caught up in the investigation meant the creditors would never be off his back in the UK. He needed to accept that and find his feet in Tenerife. The potential timeshare scheme seemed perfect if he could secure financial backing and, most importantly of all, allies on the island.

Fortunately, Tenerife was an easy place for John to impress. He was always immaculately dressed and charming. Everyone on the island had seen the news about him, and the locals loved his bright-eyed, affluent 'loadsa-money' caricature. 'This fella did Brink's-Mat – he must be loaded,' was the obvious assumption.

The landowners were willing to do deals if he was able to raise liquid assets. Police claimed Midge had been able to send in excess of £30,000 in such a short time. He had sold almost everything that wasn't nailed down: jewellery, cars, motorbikes, the lot. But it would not be enough to start the scale of development needed. John had the cash tied up in his businesses back home but, in the short term at least, he knew the police were freezing everything they could to force him back to meet detectives.

'The bastards have robbed me,' he would say. 'It's ironic given what I'm accused of.'

However, John saw lots of potential to turn around his fortunes in Playas de las Americas. Sun, sand and cheap land – it was the perfect recipe.

Without the ready cash to launch his plans alone, he set about wooing pretty much anyone and everyone he had heard of on the island for investment. John took daily Spanish classes and bought a little white van to travel the island meeting people. He set about using his charm and reputation to persuade anyone who would listen that he would make them rich.

Yet again it was amazing how much he could win people over, even with the prospect of a potential ten-year jail stretch for Brink's-Mat hanging over his head. His notoriety in some ways seemed to help. The rough diamond act worked for John, and the developers he was talking to were not naive. They had seen the millions that had poured into the Costas on the back of schemes by roguish Britons.

John would be out daily with Terry, meeting 'clients' to discuss the timeshare ideas, while I was home with the children and very little to do. I desperately missed home, and wondered whether I would ever see my beloved Coach House again. Without any money or even a passport, I was trapped and lonely.

For my husband, however, this was a time of huge opportunity. John soon seemed to be known by everyone across the island as his face was printed in the papers daily over the twists and turns back home. He was approached more and more for investment opportunities, presumably because developers believed he had all the Brink's-Mat gold. John, yet again, had been proven right. He had repeatedly been telling me: 'Keep your nerve, love – there's a silver lining to this Brink's-Mat cloud.'

Eventually, John was introduced to a man who owned pretty much all the land in southern Tenerife. The pound signs were in John's eyes before they had even shaken hands. John played down his own cashflow problem like a poker pro, and eventually struck a deal for a piece of land for himself. Finally, he could embark on his dream, and also move his money away from the authorities in Britain.

I would join John for dinners with rich and powerful Spanish businessmen. Having been home alone, worried sick, it irked me to see John being treated almost as a celebrity. He made me come along even though I was breastfeeding. It was embarrassing, as my screaming child would often disrupt the conversation over dinner. Every time I came it was the same scene, I would have to get up midway through the meal to feed Sammy in the toilets. Then I would come back to the table to a cold dinner. I had no idea why John kept insisting I was there.

A lot of deals were made around the table in those early days. The key to getting the land at cheap prices was to ensure buyers – or at least the names on the paperwork – were born and bred on the island. The lawyer suggested John should be a silent partner as far as contracts were concerned. John's main bargaining chip was that he would plough his money into the project when he retrieved all his assets after the Brink's-Mat investigation. John's ambitions would only materialise if he was able to convince people he would return their money with interest when his own riches came through. Amazingly, people trusted John and were willing to take that leap of faith with him. Within a few months, John had raised enough money to buy three derelict sites at ludicrously cheap prices; huge plots of land for close to £10,000 each. With his new business backers, the diggers began moving in within weeks.

★

While John was relishing his newfound fame, I was falling apart. It was just me, Janie and a screaming baby for most of the time. I think I was suffering postnatal depression and I desperately wanted to return home, but thought John would never allow it.

I could just about cope while we were staying at Terry McKay's home near to one of the plots John had bought, but I became even more lonely when we moved into our own small flat in the basement of a flat complex. Despite John's bulletproof optimism, for me it was grim. Our apartment was at the top of a ridiculously steep hill and there were cockroaches scuttling everywhere. I just wanted to get the children home.

Weeks would turn to months as John became the Met's most wanted. His survival strategy continued to be to make as many allies as he could in Spain. He loved playing politics and thought he might be able to stir up a diplomatic tug of war.

'I am a wronged man,' he told anyone who would listen. 'It's just the British police trying to stop me spending my money in Spain.'

I'm not sure anyone believed this, but there was certainly a delay in any cooperation with British authorities over his extradition.

John felt there was hope as other alleged villains had won shelter in Spain. Spain's Costa del Sol – once dubbed 'Costa del Crime' – had been known as a hideaway for British criminals for ten years because there were no extradition agreements with the UK. Infamous Brits to have fled to the region included Great Train robber Charlie Wilson, who was shot dead in Marbella in 1990, and Freddie Foreman, an associate of the Kray twins.

There were rumblings that the European Arrest Warrant was about to come into law but John was convinced he could persuade Spanish authorities not to cooperate with the Metropolitan Police.

'Look at all those thugs on the Costas,' he would tell local businessmen over dinner.

'You can throw away the key with that lot. The difference with me is that I'm an innocent man and I have millions of pounds of legitimate investment to plough into Tenerife.'

Despite Midge's efforts to get us money, cash was tighter than ever. It was unbelievable that people believed we had the

Brink's-Mat money. Everything was being ploughed into the new businesses and there was very little to actually live off. John didn't want anyone to know that we were struggling. We had to keep this a fierce secret as John thought it bad for business.

We were still living out of suitcases and it was very hard work. I had to climb down and back up 100 steps on a hill below the apartment every day if the girls were going to get any fresh air at all. There was also nowhere to buy the basics, let alone some meat or dinner ingredients. I was still breast-feeding. I felt weak. I had never anticipated that life in the sunshine could be so bleak. I doubted we would be able to cope like this for much longer.

With all the luxuries I'd enjoyed at the Coach House, I was well accustomed to my home comforts. Money changes you quickly and I was spoilt. My horses, stables and swimming pool suddenly seemed an awfully long way away.

Eventually Terry helped get us a nicer apartment in the resort of Puerto Del Carmen. It was so luxurious compared to our previous digs and had the use of a pool. But I was still pretty miserable, and so was Janie. We had to find her a school, even though she couldn't speak a word of Spanish. Predictably, she hated it.

After three months out there, I was at breaking point, so I confronted John, and told him I wanted to go home. 'I can't do this any more, John,' I said. Then it all came gushing out, and the tears flowed.

'I'm frightened what it might do to our baby. I need to go home.'

John was surprisingly relaxed, and agreed to help me get back to Bath. I was taken aback by his calm response – part of me had hoped he would fight to keep me there at his side, but I was relieved that I could do as I wished.

'Will this be the end of us?' I asked.

'No, we are married forever,' he said. 'I'll be back too in a few years. You'll see. My name will be cleared.'

The following morning a contact of John's picked us up and took me to the British Consulate, in Santa Cruz. The Consulate couldn't help us enough when I told them I wanted to go home with the girls. I guess they were bending over backwards because they thought I might have a valuable piece of intelligence to pass on to Scotland Yard. The officials there provided me with a temporary passport while John's solicitor arranged our flights. Given John's tense stand-off with the Met Police, I was delighted at how simple it was to fly back home.

That day is so vivid in the memory. I remember leaving the Consulate with the temporary passport, clutching Sammy and Janie. We walked into the big square in Santa Cruz and I felt a rush of elation that I was finally heading home. Janie had been such a good girl during our extended stay. She was barely 8, but she had kept me going through every long day with her exuberance. We looked around the shops for a present and I bought her a rabbit fur coat. We then sat down in the square and I gazed around at the olive trees.

'Maybe it's not bad here after all,' I thought to myself. It was much easier to think that when I knew I was escaping. Previous to that day the island had felt like my Alcatraz.

The evening before we flew home we travelled back to the Marbella Club, where John had organised some farewell drinks with a handful of our local friends. I was in good spirits, but got quite emotional as the night wore on. With a few drinks inside me, I was crying. Almost inevitably, I asked him again: 'What are we going to do, John? How will we survive this?'

John was still incredibly relaxed about the whole thing, even though we were just hours away from leaving him.

'There is absolutely nothing to worry about, darling. This is just the start of our life together. I'll get you a flight back out here in a few weeks.'

As he said that, a huge lorry chuntered past the bar. 'Look, here come the builders. These are just the foundations. You'll see. The police can't keep me down.'

Ultimately, he would be right. The long, long street with just a few derelict shops would soon become Tenerife's answer to the Las Vegas strip. John was the big man in town – the 'player' in Playas.

I was worried about being arrested as soon as the plane touched down on UK soil, but our solicitor had reassured me this was unlikely to happen with the children with me.

'It's John they want,' his lawyer said. 'You go home and get your head down.'

I should be so lucky. When I eventually got back to the Coach House, a pack of journalists were camped outside. Janie was lying down on the back seat so she wouldn't be seen or photographed. We refused to speak to any of them that night but my solicitor told them I would give a short statement at his office the next day if they left the family in peace.

After a restless night's sleep, I told the journalists: 'My husband is innocent, we have nothing to hide, and he will stay in Tenerife while he clears his name.'

The press conference didn't make much difference. The doorbell was going again from 7 a.m. onwards for days afterwards.

Photographers remained outside morning, noon and night, waiting for John to return. The press followed us everywhere from the school run to the doctor, and even to nail appointments. It was ludicrous. The attention was so intense, and I felt guilty about my children being caught up in this. My parents had arranged for Janie to go back to school in Bitton, near our home. It was amazing how quickly she readjusted. We tried to make life as normal as possible.

The neighbours were generally okay with us, and I had some good friends. But there were a few comments in the village. I remember taking Janie to the doctor's and she told me a nurse had mentioned that she 'shouldn't worry about being tarred with the same brush'. Janie told me because she didn't know what it meant, but that comment unnerved me. I wondered if they were asking her questions about John's activities.

As we settled back in, I was shocked by how much of our belongings had been sold. Midge had helped sell so much to raise the £30,000 John needed to get on his feet in Tenerife. Being such a car nut, I must admit it was galling to arrive back and find none of my cars were there. Even my MG, which I had got right at the start of our relationship, had been sold off. Terry McKay helped sort out an old banger for me.

I was up and running and, gradually, we settled back into our old routine. Eventually, I got my own passport so I could fly out to Tenerife for short trips to see John. I flew out for a brief stay with him a few weeks later. The pressure was still mounting back in Britain but John remained entirely focused on the timeshares. I met him in Puerto de la Cruz and he told me: 'You're in for one hell of a treat.'

By then he was getting all sorts of freebies because people wanted his business and believed he was not someone to trifle with. He had all sorts of friends in high places. John said one of his contacts was a friend of the King of Spain, who had a suite at the top of Tenerife's best hotel. As part of his offer for a property deal, he said we could stay there for the weekend. It was the most amazing palatial suite I had ever seen, but I was slightly put off when I went swimming and my blonde hair turned a shocking shade of green.

During one stay we let my youngest daughter run around naked because of her nappy rash. You can imagine what happened when she needed the loo. I was somewhat nervous about getting those stains out of the royal carpets!

Over the coming few months, I travelled out to see John a handful of times. Sometimes with the kids, sometimes without. With Scotland Yard unable to break the deadlock in securing an international arrest warrant, John believed he could remain a free man as long as he stayed away from airports.

After about ten months of popping over every couple of weeks, John started flying me over to Alicante instead, and we had some lovely times there. The first time I went out there, John had booked me into a first-class lounge at Heathrow. Alan, who worked around the house for us, drove me to the airport. As I arrived at the lounge I spotted Danny La Rue talking to his mother on the phone, I had always been a huge fan so was very impressed. John was waiting at the airport when I landed. I was so pleased to see him. We walked through the main square and into a saddlers, where John bought me a lovely pair of dressage gloves and a gold stick pin. We then drank sangria for hours and had a good giggle. It was the most relaxed we had been since Brink's-Mat.

After that trip, I never set foot again in Tenerife. The island had too many bad memories and John was happy to meet me elsewhere. The timeshare empire was taking off, and it suited John to keep me at arm's length.

When he was particularly busy with work, I did once ask: 'John, let me come out and help you in the office.'

But it was a half-hearted offer; I was more than happy to stay in Bath with my girls and the horses, and John was very content with this arrangement.

'No, Marnie, you stay here,' he would say. 'Make the Coach House your life. I want to keep you out of the business arrangements for your sake.'

Several years later it became clear that there was another very significant reason he didn't want me there. Unfortunately for me, John was enjoying himself a little bit too much when I wasn't by his side. It wasn't just the businessmen who were rolling out the red carpet for John. With me back in Bath, the women on the island were also fluttering their eyes at him.

The woman who made the greatest impression was Christina Ketley. I remember John talking about her even then. However, he was never very particularly flattering about her, and I thought nothing of it. Christina, a studious young brunette, was in Tenerife doing summer holiday work, and I think John initially offered her a chance to help with admin as he went about recruiting a sales team. She was about fourteen years younger than John; I didn't think they would have anything in common.

However, John told me he was keen to get Christina involved, as her parents had a lot of money to invest. I now know her parents lived a pretty ordinary life in Essex, and John clearly had ulterior motives for wanting her close. At the time, however, things were so chaotic and uncertain that I didn't even stop and wonder whether Christina was John's bit on the side. At that stage, I was pretty confident that John loved me. He told a lot of lies about his work, but I didn't think he would be able to hide what went on between us. In my eyes at least, I was still his number one.

John was so obsessed with the timeshares that I think he stopped giving the police investigation back home much thought. Instead, he was focused on assembling the most competitive and ruthless group of salesmen he could find. With the financial backing and development all but secured, John now needed to fulfil his side of the bargain – punting the timeshares to British holidaymakers. He would say: 'I need people like me – high-energy and willing to walk across hot coals to get deals.'

There was a real excitement about this side of the business. John knew everything there was to know about getting a sale. That had been the secret of his success throughout his career, from market stalls to scrap to carpets, and then to gold.

'Selling a slice of winter sun to miserable Britons? Nothing could be easier,' he told his young employees.

Many of the initial sales team were on the island working odd jobs for the holiday season. John mainly employed Brits, but I was never really allowed to get to know any of them all that well, probably because he was becoming very close with Christina and didn't want me to know.

John found the recruitment process frustrating; he was disappointed that so many people didn't share his drive for success. The Brink's-Mat police raid had really changed something in him. It had made him angry, and determined to become an even greater success.

Within months, the newspapers were reporting he had a sign in his front office in Tenerife: 'Remember the golden rule – he who has the gold makes the rules.'

7

LONDON CALLING

I think John would have happily lived as a fugitive forever. He had his development in the sun, and he would only have to deal with the girls and me when we flew out to see him every few weeks. Life was okay, to an extent, for me as well. I was glad to be back at home with the horses.

But the pressure was ramping up as the months rolled by. The Home Office was facing real heat from Scotland Yard to seek greater powers of extradition, and John's name had repeatedly come up in a string of court hearings in the UK.

Noye's trial for the John Fordham killing took place in December 1985. He had stabbed the detective eleven times and the autopsy showed that most of the wounds were inflicted when Fordham was immobile. It was a terrifying trial and I felt so sorry for Mr Fordham's wife. Noye had told jurors he had attacked the officer because he thought he was a burglar in the grounds of his home in Kent.

The jury accepted Noye's version of events and returned a shock 'not guilty' verdict on the murder charge. There were rumours the jury had been nobbled, and John fumed about the case because he knew it would eventually bring more heat on him. He knew a court would try to make out that the two of them were thick as thieves, even though they had never even met.

By killing Fordham, Noye had ensured there was no chance police would ever rest until he and all of his associates were behind bars.

To make matters worse, in February 1986, John's good friend Johnny Groves was hauled before the courts on separate charges of gold smuggling. The prosecution at Bristol Crown Court heard allegations John was involved in a plot to import £500,000 worth of gold coins into England. Johnny admitted bringing 1,800 Krugerrands worth £489,000 from Jersey to evade £73,400 duty on them. But Michael de Navarro, for the prosecution, claimed John's famous Rolls-Royce was used to bring the coins into the country. Judge Sir Ian Lewis said it would be wrong to make any finding on John's involvement, but added: 'There are suspicious circumstances.'

Then, in May 1986, Garth, Terry Patch and Noye went on trial for the Brink's-Mat gold. Also in the dock were Noye's alleged associates, Brian Reader and Tommy Adams, both of whom would become well known in their own right in later years.

The Old Bailey heard John had worked with five others in a 'simple' plot to dispose of gold bullion. For the first time, the police and prosecution had to lay their cards on the table, and I sent every cutting I could get back to John. For John, the eleven weeks of evidence would help him craft his own defence.

He was furious Garth had been tried with Noye, but he was briefed on every twist as prosecutors laid it on thick. If anything, the trial exposed how poorly police had investigated the case. They had found only eleven gold bars worth about £100,000 concealed beside the patio of Noye's home. This, John estimated, was a drop in the ocean.

It soon became clear that detectives had turned their attentions on John because of the huge amounts of money coming in and out of Scadlynn's accounts. After the Brink's-Mat robbery, £13 million was laundered through Garth and John's business account, the Crown alleged. The court was told that such was the demand for cash that their local bank, Barclays in Bedminster, had to have special deliveries of £50 notes from the Bank of England.

Meanwhile, Noye, who owned his own haulage, garage and building business, told police under questioning that he smuggled gold from Brazil and Kuwait for transmission to the Netherlands. He said he handed it over to 'frummers' – racist slang for Orthodox Jews who have interests in the jewellery industry in London's Hatton Garden neighbourhood.

Prosecutor Michael Corkery, QC, told how the scheme was controlled by Noye, a multimillionaire company director. He decided to melt down the stolen gold and sell it to dishonest dealers on the legitimate gold market. Mr Corkery said three men had since been convicted of the robbery.

'But the gold was not recovered at that stage, and the Crown say only a small amount has been recovered since,' he said. Clearly, the British government wouldn't rest until they had given John a full shake-down on home soil.

Mr Corkery then explained in public for the first time why Noye had turned to John. He said handling the stolen gold presented substantial difficulties. It weighed 3 tonnes and the bars carried identification marks. John was the only man who could make that ID vanish.

'Noye's answer to the problem smacks of simplicity,' Mr Corkery said. 'He decided to re-smelt the gold so the marks were removed, and dispose of it in small parcels in the legitimate gold market. It was decided to provide bogus documents to provide an honest background to the stolen gold. It was to be released to dishonest gold dealers with access to the honest gold market. In addition there was another plan to make more money than merely the price of the gold … Bogus documents claiming that the bullion dealer bought the gold and paid VAT at 15 per cent were to be produced.'

Corkery said the stolen gold was passed through a chain from Kent to the West Country. It began, he said, at Noye's house in West Kingsdown, where he would release small parcels of the bullion to Reader, who would take the haul back to London and pass it on to Adams at his Islington home.

Adams worked in cooperation with two men named in the charge, Wayman and Larkins, who were not before the court. 'The three were responsible for moving the gold from London to a number of collection points between London and Bristol,' Mr Corkery said.

That's when John came in. In Bristol, Chappell and Patch received the gold at Scadlynn. It seemed some of the gold ingots were melted down at Scadlynn, while some were melted down at our home. John 'cannot be found in this country,' the court heard.

I fed every day's evidence back to John. He was worried about Garth and Terry, and still annoyed by the suggestion he was working closely with Noye. He seemed pretty relaxed about his own situation, however.

As it turned out, he probably should have been more concerned. A few weeks into the trial, Spain's extradition law was on the verge of reform, enabling the Met Police to request his arrest. A well-placed Spanish police source – thanks to all those months of buttering up – warned him police were about to move in on him.

John had to hatch a new plan. He managed to order a fake Brazilian passport, and decided to try to fly out to Rio. The city was suggested by an associate, who cited the lifestyle enjoyed by Great Train Robber Ronnie Biggs. Brazil also had no extradition treaty with the UK when Biggs arrived there, in 1970.

Biggs' status as a known criminal meant he could not work, visit bars or be outside his house after 10 p.m. To make some money, Biggs' family hosted barbecues at his home in Rio, where tourists could meet Biggs and hear him recount his involvement in the robbery, which, in fact, was minor.

I think John related to that. As a fringe member himself, he would have to do all he could to save his own skin. He knew I would have found it tough, though. I was too much of a home bird.

'It will be fine, love,' he told me. 'You can come and see me whenever you want.'

John got his flight out on 28 June 1986. I can just picture his look of supreme confidence as he sat back in his seat sipping his brandy, and no doubt humming along to *Rio* by Duran Duran. But the plan terrified me. Surely no country would want to take in John Palmer, with all those negative headlines.

This time I was right. His escape plan came unstuck before his plane's wheels touched Brazilian tarmac. John didn't set a free foot in Brazil. As he looked out of the window as the long-haul flight came in to land, he saw the flashing blue lights on the ground waiting for him. He dashed to the toilet and flushed his documents down the loo, but clearly the game was up. The police boarded the flight as soon as it landed.

He couldn't understand much of what they were saying, but a translator soon filled him in on the sobering reality that he would be going back to London as soon as they could secure a safe flight. The officers took him to a Rio station, where they confirmed with Scotland Yard how he would be returned to London.

Senhor Giovanni Azevedo, one of the officers to detain John, asked: 'Are you connected to the Brinks robbery?'

John replied: 'Yes, the press has tried to accuse me of that, but I had nothing to do with it … I think I have a small problem in London but I think I can resolve it in a few weeks.'

British Embassy officials in Brazil were considering whether to question John before he surprised officers by immediately volunteering to return to London. As flights were arranged, John ended up staying three nights in the most squalid shared cell.

'There were seven of us in there, two to a single bed,' he told me. 'It was filthy, there were no lights. In the early hours one of the other prisoners started screaming.

'I had no idea what he was saying, but when I got up to look, I saw the other bloke in his bed was just lying there with his eyes open.

'I tried to shake him awake but he was dead. We screamed for a guard but nobody came. It was another six or seven hours before the body was taken away.'

After this horrifying experience in the cell, John was relieved to be heading back to London. On 2 July, John was placed on a non-stop flight, Varig 706, arriving shortly after noon at London Heathrow, where half a dozen Scotland Yard detectives boarded the plane to arrest him formally. John had been away from Britain for seventeen months. Looking calm and relaxed, he made no comment to the press as he was led through the airport. He was taken briefly to London's Snow Hill police station, and then to Kennington.

I had seen events unfold on the TV news. I felt completely powerless and horrified, but a part of me was glad that at least now John wouldn't be looking over his shoulder any longer. To his credit, John called me as soon as police allowed him to.

'Those bastards have got me, took 'em a while,' was pretty much all he said. Typical John – he sounded cool as a cucumber.

As I wept down the phone, he added: 'Really, don't worry. I know we'll be okay.'

Again, typical John.

John's capture was heralded as the start of a stream of British fugitives expelled from Spain fleeing to South America. Extradition arrangements came into force the week after he returned. Spain also passed a new aliens act, which created powers for the expulsion of foreigners.

I spoke to the police, and they agreed to let me come up to see him. My mum and stepdad drove me up to Snow Hill police station, which is a City of London police base, just around the corner from the Old Bailey. I'm not sure why John was being held there initially.

I was in bits, but as he met me in the police interview room, I was amazed by his demeanour: he even gave me a smile. Clearly, he had had enough of the constant worrying. He was shaken, clearly, but there was a sense of relief. We hugged and kissed and were allowed twenty minutes to talk across a police desk. I was horrified as he told me what had happened to him in Brazil with the fellow lag dying in his cell. It made me terrified to think what he might experience in the weeks ahead.

By this stage, John just wanted to get on with the trial. Deep down he knew this moment would eventually catch up with him. Nobody can spend their whole life looking over their shoulder.

As I left the police interview room, he shouted out at me: 'Stop worrying. Give the girls a kiss from me.'

I then rushed back inside for a final hug.

Having taken so long to get their man, police were swift in getting him before a judge. Three days after returning, John appeared before Horseferry magistrates, where Det Chief Supt Inspector Ron Smith, of Scotland Yard's special operations task force, objected to bail. Philip Alberg, John's lawyer, made no further application and John was remanded in custody until 11 July.

John had spent his first few weeks back in the UK at Wormwood Scrubs. I went to see him there on his first week. It was like something from a Charles Dickens scene: bleak, dark, filthy and hostile.

John's demeanour was now completely different, a world away from his previous Cool Hand Luke mien. He emerged in the meeting hall trembling. He looked terrified, like a caged animal. I had never seen him like this. There was thick glass between the desks, and I couldn't even give him a hug as a guard was breathing down our necks the whole time. He said they were keeping him in solitary because he was deemed such an escape risk.

I've no idea how John coped with this; it terrified me just to visit. The place was a dump and there were only murderers, rapists and terrorists on John's wing. It just showed how much authorities hated him: he was either kept in solitary or amongst the Category A crooks.

The police and CPS were clearly determined to make life as difficult as they could. John knew he needed the very best defence lawyer that money could buy. Associates told John there was only one man for the job: Henry Milner.

Henry was an incredible support, and so knowledgeable. I was confused and scared about what was going to happen, but he was the sort of chap that was always completely unfazed. He was based in London but gave me his home number for emergencies. It was a real comfort knowing I could call him, even though he was masterminding all the biggest defence cases of that time.

Henry was confident but realistic about the trial John faced. You can see right through people at these times of crisis, and it was clear he was genuine and authentic. Even now his reputation for defence work is regarded as among the very best. *Chambers Directory* remarks that 'his wealth of experience is such that he isn't just a member of the old school, he's probably the headmaster there'. And, true to form, he left no stone unturned to help John prepare for his big moment at the Old Bailey. His manner of complete self-control had a relaxing effect on John. They were a great team and that helped John for the most important day of his life – his appearance in the witness box.

Just a few weeks after John's return to the UK, Garth, Terry, Noye and Reader were all found guilty. Garth, John's beloved mate, was sentenced to ten years in jail for handling the stolen gold, and a £200,000 fine with six months to pay.

John called that evening. He was devastated. 'Poor Garth,' he sobbed. 'And he didn't even do a runner – what the hell am I looking at from the judge?'

That had been the first time I had ever heard John even consider the prospect that he might be found guilty.

Noye, meanwhile, had been as charmless as ever as he was found guilty, telling jurors, 'I hope you all die of cancer.'

As a result, jurors were promised police protection as Judge Richard Lowry told the gang: 'You enthusiastically and ruthlessly pursued dishonest profit.'

Noye got fourteen years, and the judge said: 'The gold stolen in the robbery may well have been vastly more than the robbers expected, but it was of little use to them until it could be converted into cash. In a manner not revealed by Noye, he became in league with the robbers. At a time when it was hoped detection would be avoided, the gold was released and sold and became cash.'

I wasn't at the sentencing but I do remember reading that Reader's wife, Lynn, shouted at her husband: 'I will wait for you, Brian.'

She later denied saying those words; it wasn't her style to make a scene. However, it did made me wonder what I would do or say should John be jailed. After those convictions, it really wasn't looking good for my husband.

John called me again a few days later. He was downcast, but determined to stay resolute about his own chances of winning over the jury when he appeared before them. His solicitor had clearly been on to him with a pep talk.

The long wait to face trial affected him hugely. He became very paranoid as seven more months rolled by before he was in the dock. I think this was all part of the plan for the police. Prosecutors said they needed the time because the other case was so fresh in the public's mind.

During that gap, police went into overdrive to retrieve the gold. Officers from the Flying Squad and other specialist units, including the Yard's criminal intelligence team C11, investigated the possibility that properties were bought to conceal the money and, in some cases, cash from the proceeds was used as collateral to generate money for legitimate business interests. It was clear that officers suspected John's timeshare businesses in Tenerife were, at least in part, funded by the gold.

'Dirty liars,' John told me over the phone. 'This is their ruse to get Spanish police to cooperate. I earned every penny I've spent there.'

For a short while, Garth had been at the same jail, and I would travel up to see John with Garth's wife, Joan. She was a good friend and we were both utterly committed to supporting our men. I don't know how she kept it together after Garth went down. Her resolve was incredible.

After he was remanded formally ahead of his trial, John was sent to HMP Brixton. His treatment by the screws was so much better compared with Belmarsh, where he had been held after his arrest. John was afforded some luxuries, as he remained innocent until proven otherwise. In those days, you could bring suspects awaiting trials all sorts, and John would always tell me to bring roast dinners.

I was travelling backwards and forwards to London twice a week, sometimes three times. I took Janie and generally left Sammy with my mum. As well as a roast, we would take him snacks, magazines, £10 for a phone card, batteries for his radio and a clean tracksuit to wear.

Despite the improvement in his treatment behind bars, I was worried sick about John; he wouldn't see much daylight for around six months. During that time, I couldn't help but wonder whether my husband would ever be freed. In the outside world, Brink's-Mat was still the biggest story around at the time. Everyone was talking about it, and nobody had a profile like John's. The Met Police were desperate to get him convicted.

I believed 100 per cent that he was innocent, but of course I was worried. There was no denying that the Brink's-Mat gold had gone through the smelting works, even though John didn't know where those ingots had come from. As time wore on, I brushed myself down and convinced myself the truth would finally out. I stood by my man. That was never in doubt.

In March 1987, John finally appeared at the Old Bailey, that famous old court near Fleet Street, in central London. This was one of the biggest trials since the Krays appeared in those docks in the late 1960s.

John stood in the dock, arms behind his back, looking down at his feet as the charge was read out. He looked smart, but there were huge bags under his eyes. The exhaustion was from the months of waiting with nothing to do but think and worry. However, John thrived on company, so there was something he actually relished about the trial getting under way. At last, he could get his game face on. At the very least, he was assured of a bit of a buzz in the weeks that followed.

My husband appeared in the dock with a young man called Christopher Weyman, of Holborn, London. He was a go-between, a contact of Noye's. Weyman and John had never set eyes on each other before. Both denied conspiracy to handle stolen gold and evasion of VAT payable on it.

I can remember fixing my stare at John, just willing him to convince the jury of his innocence. I knew John always believed he could charm his way out of any situation. As it turned out, his efforts at his Old Bailey trial in 1987 were Oscar-worthy.

As we had feared, John was depicted at the trial as a close friend of Noye, a magnet for unwanted attention. In fact, there was no link at all. John was ice-cool under pressure in the dock; butter wouldn't melt.

The prosecution claimed between June 1984 and June 1985, John and Garth sold £13 million worth of gold, accompanied by bogus invoices for its original purchase, provided by a Hatton Garden dealer named Costantino, now dead. I knew full well that John wasn't making anywhere near that sort of money. Where on Earth were the police suggesting it all went?

The Crown went on to claim invoices were necessary to give 'a bogus legitimacy' to the gold, and Scadlynn used a small branch of Barclays in Bristol for regular cash transactions in the apparent buying and selling of it.

'Between £100,000 and £200,000 per day were being drawn out,' said Nicholas Purnell QC, for the prosecution. 'In order to cope they had to contact the Bank of England distribution department to make arrangements for extra cash.'

The money was paid out in new £50 notes, some of which were traced, and found to bear Weyman's fingerprints.

There were so many ups and downs with the case. I was relieved when the prosecution admitted our holiday in Tenerife was booked 'quite innocently and without forethought ... It is not suggested for one moment by the Crown that he planned it. It just happened it coincided with the police swoop on his premises.'

But my blood was boiling by day two as Purnell said John was the 'most shadowy figure' in the whole gang, suggesting my husband had in some way deliberately negotiated the sale of the gold back to Johnson Matthey, the victims of the raid. I was absolutely furious when he said John was the main architect of this recycling operation. I wanted to stand up in court and scream. Purnell made us out to be criminal masterminds, having filled his opening statement with exaggeration on detail to increase the sense of drama. He said John melted the gold in a furnace 'by a horsebox in the back bushes at his home'. John was no angel, but to describe him as the head of this complex chain of criminal acts seemed perverse to me.

The money they claimed was going through John's accounts was pie in the sky. He was doing well, really well. But I saw

with my own eyes that the most John ever had in savings was
£50,000. The rest was spent as quickly as he could earn it.

Then, on day three, came the moment when I realised for
sure that the Crown was lying. The jury was told a telephone
code book with Noye's number written on it was found in
John's home. Police claimed this piece of evidence proved
John was a liar after he previously denied that he knew Noye.
In fact, this 'evidence' offered us a huge opportunity to undermine the case against him.

A handwriting expert and my mother were called to look
at the writing in court. Both said the scrawl definitely wasn't
John's handwriting. We couldn't prove that the police had
planted it, but we could at least prove John had not written
down that number. This was our turning point.

'We've got a fighting chance,' John said me. 'It's a small
chance, but we're fighting.'

Then came John's defining moment, his turn in the witness
box. I was too stressed to take in a lot of what was being said, but
I remember him calmly admitting that he kept a smelter, and
even that Johnson Matthey was one of his major customers.

However, John explained convincingly that he had believed
the gold he was selling was from a deal involving a firm called
Smith Finance, involving 20 tonnes of gold. He told the court:
'Obviously, there was a lot of gold coming in. I just wanted to
check it was 100 per cent legal. At the time I was told it was
the Smith Finance deal which caused the influx.'

The court was also told about his activities in Tenerife. John
told the jury he had set up the timeshare quickly from the
sale of cars and belongings – but he had made nothing like
the figures being suggested in court. The Crown claimed the
business was already worth £3 million. That was ridiculous,
but it was difficult for John to pull this claim apart, as police

knew full well his game in Tenerife had been to make people believe he had more cash than was actually the case. The diggers were in the ground on new developments, but they were working on a promise from John, rather than actual pay cheques. Meanwhile, all the assets were frozen in the UK. We were far from millionaires at that precise point, and we definitely didn't have the Brink's-Mat profits.

However, John's trump card in court was that he could tear the Met Police timeline of evidence to shreds. They had alleged that in 1984 he had smelted down unmarked gold for Scadlynn, but John clarified that he had left the company in early 1984, before this deal could have taken place. He looked each and every juror in the eye, summoning all the charm that had already got him so far in life.

'I may have touched the gold, melted it down even ... But I didn't know where it was from.'

As the case reached summing up, everything hung in the balance. I knew he was innocent, but John didn't want me there because of all the press attention. For once, I had to ignore his orders: I had to be there to see on the day of reckoning.

We were both so tense, especially when Judge Richard Lowry was told of a suspected approach to a juror over the weekend. He had ordered a guard for the jury for the rest of the deliberations.

Our prayers were answered on 1 April 1987. John was acquitted unanimously. I watched down from the public gallery and was barely able to speak as he was cleared of any involvement in the case, and also of tax evasion charges. The sense of relief was incredible.

John swaggered from the dock and blew a kiss at those jurors and mouthed, 'Thank you.' I was jumping around in ecstasy, but it didn't stop me from feeling a pang of shame as

John then sauntered towards a row of detectives and flicked two fingers at them. It was such a stupid, arrogant thing to do. John would be a marked man from that moment on, whether he kept his nose clean or not.

The jury clearly thought he was a nicer bloke than they did the officers giving evidence against him. The press would speculate that John had nobbled the jury. But the media was wrong, he had instead cast a spell on them with his charm.

John was swept away and went to see his legal team. I knew he would be some time as he needed to be signed out and have his acquittal confirmed. I was going to join them but then thought to myself that he would want to celebrate back in Bath. I dashed out of the court, ghosted past the press pack, and into a waiting car. I had a smile like the Cheshire cat as we dashed back down the M4. It felt like the beginning of a new life, and I couldn't wait to see John and celebrate.

Henry Milner told reporters his client had not returned after the raid in January 1985 'because he did not want to remain in custody for over a year waiting trial, which happened to various defendants who stood trial last year'. Henry said the family 'were over the moon. His wife always believed in his innocence.'

8

MONEY TALKS

John was delighted to be free, but he knew he was finished doing business in Britain. The threat of prison had gone away but he remained on a list of fifty men facing High Court actions to trace proceeds of the robbery. The first writ was issued the previous July. Similar actions were also being pursued through the courts in a number of foreign countries.

I eventually got back to the Coach House to the biggest pack of press imaginable. I had only seen this number of journalists once before – on TV, for Princess Diana. We could see the flashbulbs from a mile away. It was absolutely ridiculous.

We had big electric gates and Rottweilers prowling around our grounds, yet journalists were still risking their own limbs by jumping over the wall and dashing to our front door to pop a note through offering crazy amounts of money for interviews.

The *News of the World* was the most persuasive paper. We had several letters from them. John had told me he wouldn't be doing an interview for £1 million. Yet, even when I relayed this to the reporters, they kept coming back.

Having sorted out his legal business, John got back to the Coach House an hour or so after me. He was typically resourceful and spotted the press pack from about a mile away. He told his driver to pull over around the corner. He then walked through all the fields behind the estate and came in through the back door.

'We're going to have some party tonight,' he said. 'If we can survive that, we can survive anything.'

Despite previously saying he would never speak to the papers again, he told me to go outside and tell the press he wasn't back tonight, but we would speak to them tomorrow.

We enjoyed a drink together and then a quiet party with the small group of friends who had stuck by us. The champagne flowed into the early hours. It was complete jubilation and we danced until we dropped.

The next morning I woke up early. 'Goldfinger gets away with it' was the lead item on the morning TV news.

The press were gathering outside our home all night. We had agreed to give a statement at 11 a.m. I was hung-over, but very happy. I quickly got dressed and snuck out around the back for a pint of milk from the local newsagent. The smile was soon wiped off my face, because as I handed the money over the counter, I noticed a pile of newspapers. Blazing across the front of a tabloid: 'Goldfinger's Mistress'.

It had a picture of a brunette woman. Without even reading the story, I assumed it was Christina, who had been working in the Tenerife office. I ran out of the shop screaming.

I felt humiliated and deeply, deeply hurt. As I was caring for his children, John was seducing his secretary – and eventually sleeping with her. What a cliché. I had been standing by him through this entire ordeal like a fool. Had this seedy little union continued even when he was locked up at Brixton?

It beggared belief. Predictably, John said he didn't know the woman and it was a load of lies. But he would have said anything to calm me down, as we had to face the press.

I was inconsolable. There was no way I wanted to stand in front of all those journalists for his press conference. But he begged me to be at his side, and eventually I agreed, just so we could get on with life again.

It was Easter and I remember one of the reporters gave us a Terry's All Gold Easter egg. I held it for the photos and tried to grin and bear it. That picture has been printed again and again. I still don't know how I managed to fight back the tears.

'I am staying here with my wife – what else is there to say?' he told the journalists. I just stood there trying to keep my emotions in check.

During the press conference, John said the Coach House, as one of his assets, had been frozen by legal action taken by Brink's-Mat insurers, but he said he did not accept that the gold he had been asked to melt down was from Brink's-Mat. He had made no profit and said, 'I am under no obligation to pay a penny.'

It should have been the happiest time of our lives but we were arguing relentlessly about the affair. He denied everything, but I was fuming with him, completely besides myself with pain after putting up with all his stress. What angered me most was the thought that he was seeing her during his time inside waiting to be tried.

That was Friday. By the Monday he was flying out to Tenerife, back to the building site to direct his troops. His big dream – the timeshare empire – was already up and running. Now nothing could stop him.

John had made the most of his time during his wait to walk free from Her Majesty's Pleasure. Midge had helped sell off almost every unnecessary British asset, including his shops. I was simply relieved there was never any suggestion of getting rid of the Coach House. John, meanwhile, was spending every spare minute scrawling down notepads full of ideas for development across the island. Even after he was freed, he would sit in the kitchen for hours with pencil and paper finalising those plans for hotels in Playas de las Americas.

John would eventually be forced to pay a substantial sum to loss adjusters acting for Brink's-Mat. I was still worried about future proceedings; there was no way police were going to let John off the hook so easily. We were warned Lloyd's Insurance would spend years dogging anyone vaguely connected with the gold. By 1990, John was targeted for £360,000 in settlement of a civil action even though he had been found innocent. As the debts piled up, his only answer was to make money faster than the lawyers could take it.

John knew the Brink's-Mat legacy could be turned to his advantage. He was a hero of the underworld now, and he was willing to embrace that if it helped him make money. He wasn't keen on the nickname Goldfinger, but a shady reputation did you no harm in those days on an island like Tenerife. John, oozing with charisma and confidence after his court victory, was becoming so popular. I hope he savoured every moment, considering he would eventually be one of the most hated men across Europe!

Initially, I chose to turn a blind eye to the affair, or any of his apparent philandering. After the stress of the court drama, I was simply weary of the strife. With two girls to look after, I had to protect my future. I had lost my respect for him over the reports of the affair but John didn't care. He was in the clear so far as court was concerned. Nobody was getting in the way of his plans now, least of all me.

Midge was to thank for helping John get on his feet again. The older brother was a successful man in his own right, and was always willing to lend John cash. Once John was up and running, the progress was breathtaking. Within five years, by 1990, he was investing £5 million in 450 timeshare villas capable of earning him £72 million. It appeared he was plucking figures out of the air and making businessmen open their chequebooks.

Whether in work or at play, John had the most amazing can-do attitude. He dealt with the big moneymen and developers while his small team of salesmen would do the hard bit: pounding the streets and wearing out shoe leather to find punters interested in timeshares.

Obviously, we had been doing well before Brink's-Mat. The Coach House, the three jewellery shops, the Range Rover in the drive and the lovely holidays were all bought through sheer hard work. However, everything moved up a notch after the bullion landed on our doorstep. Since the trial, John had been dubbed 'Goldfinger' by the media. With such a high profile, he felt he had a point to prove: he needed to be bigger and more successful than he ever had been.

Now he was officially an innocent man, John no longer had to be cloak and dagger about securing property deals. The Island Village Management Ltd was set up at the Commercial Register of Santa Cruz de Tenerife in March 1989. The document listed John as 'jeweller' and even included his British passport number B343169 with domicile as The Coach House, adding that he was 'the unique administrator'. This was so significant for him. He was a completely legitimate businessman.

However, Tenerife was like a Wild West island where no rules applied. People were moving in with big ideas but little legitimate investment. You could get away with things, probably owing to the fact civilisation was relatively young compared to most of the Western world. John's ambition to set up Europe's biggest timeshare operation for British holiday-makers was within reach.

In this Thatcherite era of entrepreneurship, yuppie culture was de rigueur. And the thought of owning your own property overseas – even if just for a couple of weeks a year – was glamorous. John believed timeshares would appeal most to young businessmen in the London commuter belt. For once he was wrong. In fact, the vast majority of investors were retired folk looking to spend their hard-earned life savings.

All timeshare deals must relate to a specific time and property, include a minimum ten-day cooling-off period and the deal must be for at least thirty-six months. There was never any guarantee that a timeshare would be a good deal – the value of the property may fall and you could have problems reselling it. However, in those days, most people – including John – believed the property market would keep ballooning and never burst.

He had plans to expand all across the island. To do that, he needed to sell the timeshares as quickly as possible, mostly off plan. Tenerife's Tourism and Transport Board, the government body on the Canary Islands, accepted these terms, and were happy to recommend John as operator of the Island Village complex.

John was hiring as many people as he could find to support his timeshare expansion.

He assembled a team of salespeople you would have been more likely to find in a car showroom than on a remote island. These men and women were like candidates for Sir Alan Sugar's *The Apprentice*. They were hard-nosed, young and ambitious.

Within months, John had a staff of almost 100; they would eventually be selling properties faster than they could build them. From the start, the timeshares were being sold before the developments were built. Investors were told 'get in now, before the prices rocket'. John was making millions within a year of walking free.

The business was going better than he could have dreamed, but there were worries from the start that he would need to keep his unruly group of sales staff in check.

The sales staff partied as hard as they pitched; John needed a right-hand man to make sure they were behaving. Out of the blue, he hired Mohammed 'Mo' Derbah, an ambitious young Lebanese man with top connections in the diamond trade across Africa and beyond.

'Mo' had been looking for a new opportunity in Europe, having failed to find work in Germany and Czechoslovakia. I'm not sure how he met John, but in terms of business, the pair were a perfect match. Mo, 25, told John he would consider any work he could offer him. He was bowled over when John said he should join him at HQ, as the firm's head of security.

I remember asking people about him. One close associate was very nervy and said 'he wasn't to be trusted'. But John insisted he would be okay, and tried to reassure me by saying he had met his mum. He even flew Mo over to meet us all for lunch. He was charm personified. Now I could see why the pair of them liked each other.

My husband was impressed by Mo's drive and ambition. I think a part of him thought he could mould him in the same way as his brother Midge had done with him.

For most of the 1990s, John's new No. 2 helped him run his empire. Mo would help organise John's representatives, barking out the orders as they were sent into the streets to drum up business. Mo was all charm when it suited, but he saw his role as John's 'bad cop' should any of his employees step out of line.

He ended up becoming a ruthless operator, a henchman with his finger in all of John's pies. It allowed my husband to do as he pleased. With his lieutenant running day-to-day affairs, John was left with almost no choice but to enjoy his cash.

The pair of them were a force to be reckoned with for nine years until they fell out when Mo was arrested. Soon wild claims emerged in the press suggesting Mo was a good deal more menacing than just a no-nonsense businessman. It turned out John trusted Mo too much. According to reports in Spain, Mo was developing his own enterprises behind his boss's back. There were even unproven allegations in the newspapers of money laundering on behalf of international mafias, and running protection rackets.

However, in the early 1990s, all was sweet for John. He was undeniably the real deal as far as his underworld status was concerned. The timeshares, the jewellery businesses and the properties were running themselves, and I lost count of the amount of investments connected to his empire. There were so many businesses, so many developments, that even John struggled to keep up.

9

CASH RULES

John was happy again and our relationship began to heal – for a couple of years at least. John was coming back to the Coach House every weekend. He loved routine and we would always go out for a meal every night, often at the Royal Crescent Hotel and Spa in Bath. We would roll up at the entrance, hand the key to the valet, and wander into the entrance like royalty. Every time it was like being in a film.

Lewis, the restaurant manager, always made a great fuss of us. Like clockwork, he would welcome us with whisky sours and then ask us if we fancied our normal £150 Bordeaux wine with our meal.

'Yes, Chateau Palmer of course,' John would say with a smirk.

We always had a giggle over that wine, especially when our fellow diners would ask whether we owned the winery in southern France. Of course we didn't, but it was flattering that people even thought we could afford such a place.

Our other weekend ritual was Sunday lunch with the girls at the lovely Hunstrete House, in the pretty village of Pensford, near Bath, or Manor House Hotel, Castle Combe. Sometimes

John would take us in the helicopter. There was a lawn outside for us to land on.

This was such a different John from the one I had first met in the 1970s. John was rough round the edges, but he started to look like a refined gentleman. He always left a huge tip for staff and treated everyone he met so well.

Money suited him. I did fancy him in the designer get-up. His black hair shimmered with spray tonic and I cut his hair every third weekend. He would smell delicious in Chanel Pour Monsieur and wear some wonderful clothes: Armani, Versace, YSL, Valentino and Gucci.

John didn't need to go shopping for it. We were such good clients of Christopher Barry, our tailor in Bath, that he would send us a selection regularly. They knew his size and previous buys so all I needed to do was just say: 'John will have a navy suit, black trousers, two pairs of shorts, three shirts …'

The shop never got it wrong. It was all paid for on John's gold American Express card. No limit, of course.

Whenever I went shopping, John would hand me a wad of cash. I generally came back with a small handful of change for him. It made him laugh. He would always ask: 'Where on Earth is the rest? Did you buy the whole shop?'

As the 1990s rolled by, John presided over a labyrinth of interconnected companies. The newspapers would eventually round up his estimated worth at £300 million. This, the reports said, made him Britain's richest gangster by far, and 105th on *The Sunday Times* Rich List — equal with the Queen. I think that figure was hugely exaggerated, but it made a neat headline. And let's not beat around the bush, John was indeed a very rich man.

Money was spent like it was no object; to keep us occupied, we had more toys than an Arab sheikh. John started hiring a private jet, treating the Tenerife project like it was an easy commute. He flew out from Bristol on a Monday morning and arrived back on a Friday. He would also buy me anything I wanted. I was hopping backwards and forwards on our jet from the private hangar at Bristol Airport to wherever I fancied.

The money opened up a new world to us, but with our working-class backgrounds, people certainly saw us coming; 'nouveau riche', as we were no doubt branded behind our backs.

Understandably, John was paranoid about his money being confiscated or stolen. John never trusted the banks. I don't think he ever walked into a branch again after Barclays Bedminster dropped him and Garth in it over Brink's-Mat.

'Fool me once, shame on you; fool me twice, shame on me,' he said.

Instead, he made sure we kept cash, instead of using the banks all the time. He would keep huge wads in his pockets, and keep a lot of his savings under the cobbles in the stables at the Coach House. There was very little risk of us getting burgled as by then it was more secure than Fort Knox. He had cameras all over the place.

John was also paranoid about our personal safety and there were weapons hidden at various spots. His properties were littered with the latest security cameras on every corner. Sometimes I suspected he used them to keep an eye on me, as well as potential intruders. John's security staff patrolled the grounds, as did the Rottweilers.

Looking back, we were at our most extravagant between 1990 and 1998. During those golden years, John was spending money like it was going out of fashion. With the day-to-day running of the business in the capable hands of Mo, he pursued hobbies only the richest playboys can afford. He bought a French chateau simply so he could drink fine wines and extended his collection of classic cars as 'investments'. Between 1990 and 1993, he trained as a helicopter pilot and got his full plane licences. John wasn't book smart but he was irritatingly good at picking things up quickly.

In 1993 he bought a Squirrel helicopter, and later upgraded to a Robinson R44. They were kept in a huge shed at the Coach House which he built with his friends. Flying was a great love of his. He was in advanced talks at one stage about selling off his timeshare empire and investing with a Madeira-based company offering cheap helicopter transits. He thought there was real potential for the people wanting to make short hops, not least after he nearly missed his mum's funeral because of horrendous traffic on the M5. I remember shrieking with terror as he drove at 100mph up the hard shoulder. We only just made it to the church in time for John to carry the coffin in with his brothers. John was mortified.

There were the odd mishaps as John indulged his appetite for fun. He marked out a helipad in front of a huge lake he had dug out in our garden. However, that patch of land was used so much for his helicopter that the pad eventually collapsed into the water. His helicopter and the shed wobbled tantalisingly close to falling in, too. John was fuming, but I thought it was all hilarious.

The private jets were kept in his own vast hangar at Bristol Airport. They were quite a sight, and the thrill of boarding 'Air Force John' never left you. We could be out of the house in Bath and in the air within an hour. All the jets were so luxurious. Our main pilot, Rex, knew how to look after us. John paid a fortune to the lease company in Sweden. We flew absolutely everywhere, even across the Atlantic. Initially we leased a Learjet, then, a couple of years later, we added a larger Gulfstream.

On board they were both wonderful, decked out in beautiful leather, with champagne on tap. The pilots were always great fun, discreet and hugely patient with John, who was backwards and forwards from the UK like a yo-yo.

The only times we joined chartered flights was to get on Concorde. We regularly used that beautiful bird to fly to America and the Caribbean. I always booked all four seats at the back – it was the one spot where you really felt the raw thrust of that amazing jet.

Between 1990 and 1998, we had at least seven trips on Concorde to Barbados. The food, beaches and lifestyle were just something else. At the same time we were travelling all over Europe at the drop of a hat. We had a particularly memorable stay in Venice for Sammy's eighth birthday. We stayed in the most expensive hotel on St Mark's Square, and it was magical. We went everywhere and anywhere: the Caribbean, Marbella, Ibiza, Menorca and Palma. I was addicted to sunny getaways.

I was booking so many trips that I did make the occasional blooper with arrangements. Christmas 1989 particularly sticks in the mind. We decided to fly out to Florida on one of the few years when it was hit by snow. The hotel we arrived at was a dump, and I had a meltdown, thinking I had ruined Christmas, but John was determined to rescue our trip. He spent hours in our dingy room, phoning almost every hotel in the area. The Christmas Eve irony wasn't lost on us – that there was no room at any of the inns! Eventually, he hailed us a cab and told the driver to take us to the most expensive hotel in the state. After several more hours of negotiation we ended up with the best suite at the Miami Hyatt-Regency Hotel. We stayed there over Christmas and New Year overlooking the vast golf course. John had clearly paid a few people off, but I was so impressed and grateful to him for turning things around. It was yet another example of why he was so successful in life; he could charm anyone's socks off.

John came on so many holidays, but was always checking in on work, and arranging deals. His brown leather briefcase came everywhere with him, as did his mahogany-trimmed mobile phone with gold detail. His most important possession of all was his address book, with all of his telephone numbers. His network was vast, but he never worked out how to save the numbers on his phone. He was forever doing deals as we rushed through airports to board our plane. He would usually stay on the phone for as long as possible while the plane took off.

On one holiday to Verden, in Lower Saxony, Germany, disaster struck as we arrived at the hotel and he realised he had lost his briefcase. John paid in cash wherever he went; it would have had tens of thousands inside. He sprinted out into the road next to the promenade and hailed a cab to the airport. Fortunately, it was still on the seat in the terminal where he had been sitting three hours earlier. He was so lucky. These days, even if it hadn't been pinched, the bag would have prompted a security alert, and, more than likely, the bomb disposal team. We had been in Germany to see my horse compete in the European Dressage Championship. I was amazed we got there in time.

We also had a nervy journey travelling to and from Miami in the mid 1990s. We had taken John's Gulfstream but fuel was running low and then we ended up flying almost into the eye of a storm. The jet ended up diverting all the way north to Quebec for refuelling. The weather was terrible and I begged the pilot, Rex, not to take off again. I was as white as a sheet.

We would have many holidays. There were three or four Christmases at the Gleneagles resort in Scotland. Neither of us played golf, but it was a lovely place, and very festive if you got snow. We would fly up in our jet and John would join us a few days later when he had wrapped up business. Our rooms were about £1,000 a night each, and we were very indulgent. We would have a raucous time of it, drinking posh Scotch whisky and dancing. They put on the most spectacular show for us, and the girls loved it. One year, we dressed as Victorian-era aristocracy.

John was very generous during our stays there. One Christmas Eve he bought Janie's boyfriend a suit so he could join us for dinner. Then, during our meal, he bought a £180 glass of whisky. The waiters were so excited about it that he ordered them both a glass too. Dinners were always rounded off with the most expensive Cuban cigars available. John just loved the show of it all.

The staff treated us all like royalty, probably because John was tipping so heavily. He loved pleasing those around him. Here we go, I thought … yet more members of the John fan club. But on that very same trip I remember him going bonkers – just because I had taken a photo of him wearing my shower cap in the bathroom. It was sometimes like living with two different men.

Then there was John's most famous indulgence of all: the *Brave Goose of Essex*. The papers said he spent £6 million buying it, but I knew that was nonsense. He got hold of it as part of a property deal. I think he paid less than £100,000 in cash. The boat was simply wonderful; beautifully understated, yet luxurious. However, I do remember being somewhat underwhelmed when I first saw it because it was moored next to a Russian oligarch's superyacht.

'Oh well, size isn't everything, John,' I joked, much to his displeasure.

I ended up loving that boat; trips on the *Goose* were my favourite holidays of all. We would go out around ten times a year. It was so peaceful, even John was happy and content when we were out at sea with nothing to do but sleep, eat, fish and play board games. I bought John a gold-plated Scrabble board and Monopoly set. It was the most gorgeous thing and we used it every holiday.

We could sleep up to a dozen guests on the boat and it had a staff of around six or seven men. However, I only enjoyed staying on the boat with very close family. Generally I would fly in with Diana or the girls to meet the boat in Spain as John never wanted me near the business in Tenerife. I was happy to keep my nose out of it.

John and the captain would make sure the boat was always stocked to the brim; you would never need to leave. We had a vast drinks cabinet in the cabin, and we would get in Moët & Chandon by the case, and keep everyone topped up with some of John's favourite brandy and whisky.

John was always a generous, welcoming host, whoever we had on there. He was always trying to make everyone laugh, including the children. He would wander around in ladies' wigs or put on a weird fancy dress. How could we believe that John was one of Britain's most notorious gangsters when he was stood in front of us making a clown of himself?

The *Brave Goose* also kept John busy. There were always so many invoices to pay, and maintenance to sort out. However, it was more a hobby than a job for John.

He and the captain, a burly Dutchman called William, didn't always see eye to eye, but he and the crew eventually became like extended family. There were endless wind-ups.

William was a huge character. He loved the luxuries in life, and was forever tucking into steaks or the best wines. He was in his mid-50s, and had a Filipino bride in her early 20s.

I remember one morning in the summer of 1997, I woke up to hear William announcing on the Tannoy loudspeaker that

'Lady Di has died'. It was the nickname he used for my close friend, Diana. I cried out in horror and buzzed Diana's cabin but got no reply. I then ran to the front of the boat, and was relieved to see her sitting in the lounge. Needless to say, William was talking about the death of Diana, the Princess of Wales.

John was generally at his best when he was on that boat, away from it all. Especially if he had left his cocaine at home. Drugs were becoming an issue for him. The first time I saw him doing coke was in around 1992. John had just flown back to the West Country, and we were looking forward to spending the weekend together. I walked into the kitchen at the Coach House, and there he was, bold as brass, snorting a line.

It may sound relatively ordinary and mundane these days, but I found it a real shock. I banned it from the home, but, as the months wore on, he was taking it relentlessly. You could always tell. His behaviour was exaggerated, he would sweat and he had mood swings. Worst of all, it made him very volatile.

I repeatedly yelled at him about it. We would argue about the drugs and, latterly, other women. I just hated the impression it gave Janie, who was now old enough to work out what was going on. I never wanted the girls to know he took that filthy stuff, but he did a terrible job hiding it. You would see the marks from where he had snorted a line in the bathroom on the boat, or notice his nose was running.

During the drug and women worries, I distracted myself with material pleasures. There were some cars to die for in the boom years. He bought me a brand new top of the range 911 with all the extras from Dick Lovett, a showroom in Swindon. It was the most gorgeous car and I would only use it on very special occasions. When I eventually sold it seventeen years later, it had just 22,000 miles on the clock. I think the buyer got the bargain of a lifetime. He also added a beautiful 1960s

Ferrari, a rare 'Gullwing' Mercedes, another classic E-type Jaguar, and ordered an Aston Martin Vanquish.

Those cars were for his enjoyment at home, rather than use. The cars we used on a day-to-day basis became generally quite low-key: a Mercedes or a BMW was typical. He wasn't interested in being spotted in a flashy red sports car. Our drivers were always there, waiting to take us wherever we wanted. There were plenty of shopping jaunts; friends and I loved being whisked up to London to mooch around Harrods.

John spoiled me with my favourite things, from clothes to cars to horses. At the Coach House we had exotic fish and a whole menagerie to admire. In Tenerife, he stocked his office pond with rare albino frogs. When they died, he put in piranhas. Only the most bloodthirsty survived in that place. It was almost prophetic!

The horses were always my first passion, and also my escape from any marriage stress. I competed in many dressage events. Lee Groves, who worked for us both, helped with training and driving for the events. When it came to events, I wondered at first whether people would take us seriously. I imagined they would read about John, hear my West Country accent, and make up their minds straight away that I was an imposter, but it wasn't like that. I won rosettes, and it was wonderful!

John bought me a lovely horsebox so I could travel further afield. Initially he would drive me to events, but as he became busier, Lee ferried me everywhere instead. I first started winning on a horse called Dream. We then moved on to a 3-year-old named Star. He was gorgeous; we kept him in Verden and he won his class.

With both my girls at school and John away for most of the week, I loved investing all my energy in looking after all our animals. By 1995, I had four horses, was competing several times a week, and I had bought two Harris's hawks, which needed to be exercised every day. We also had an amazing salt-water fish tank set up in the office. It was a vast thing.

Yes, I had marriage problems, but I didn't need reminding that life overall was pretty damn good. I could go wherever I wanted, and I had as much money as I needed to pay for it. I was also extremely proud of my equestrian career.

From the outside, my set-up was enviable, but I was living in a bubble, trying to ignore the little telltale signs that John was up to no good. At his best he was so loveable, generous, hard-working and endearingly chaotic. But at his worst he was deceitful, womanising and ultimately violent. Despite all those years of wealth, I probably would have swapped it for a quiet life in the suburbs away from John.

The drugs really brought out John's nasty side, and there were some horrible rumours about his increasingly wild behaviour. One hotel in Los Cristianos claimed John had been seen holding a woman by her ankles from a balcony. I heard all about it from one of his sales managers.

It was a horrifying thought. Of course, John denied everything, but I knew what he was like in one of his cocaine-addled tempers. It wouldn't have surprised me if he had ended up getting into a fight after taking a woman back to a room.

He could also be very two-faced, and change his mind about people. Countless friends were suddenly dropped. There was a couple we were very close to for years, but one morning John blurted out that they were grasses. I followed orders to cut off all ties with the pair of them. Yet then, within a few months, John was going to see the couple again and they were doing business together. All it did was left me out in the cold. John let them believe it was me who had created the rift. I had no idea why the sudden change of mind, but that was typical of John. He was a natural Machiavelli, always in control, and a master of pitting one person against another, even when there was no obvious gain. It was the way he did business.

10

THE DOWNFALL

Power, pressure, ego and drugs: they were the ingredients of a deadly cocktail. Having stood by my man for decades, he had lost my trust, and I hated his lifestyle. By the mid-1990s, John had started to see himself as a God. He was untouchable.

John was always confident, but now he was arrogant. His business associates were all yes men. The money was rolling in, the timeshare sales were going through the roof, but somehow it wasn't enough for John. He was taking silly risks. Initially I blamed the drugs; Tenerife was awash with cocaine by the mid 90s, and my husband was taking it morning, noon and night.

He was irrational and seemed to be losing control of his sales staff. Complaints of heavy-handedness were piling up. Sales teams chasing commission were resorting to extreme pressure tactics, hassling holidaymakers as they sunbathed on the beaches. Meanwhile, investors were questioning why it was taking so long for developments to finish.

I hadn't set foot on Tenerife since the Brink's-Mat trial but I would always try to sneak an ear on John's phone calls to make sense of it all.

I remember him shouting on his mobile phone as he looked out to sea on the *Brave Goose* one summer. He yelled at one of his managers: 'You can't do this. Some of these developments haven't even been agreed, and yet we're selling them. We'll have the law all over us.'

Sometimes I think he would say things for effect because he knew I was listening. But I did get the impression he didn't approve of some of the tactics used to generate sales. He couldn't complain too much though; he was happy to take the money.

He also had no excuse for not being across it. He was the boss. He was the main man who had set up his staff on commission to ensure they would walk across hot coals to get deals done. But as the business took off, so too did his appetite for cocaine. He was also too busy with his other lovers to care.

I have no doubt the drugs were clouding his judgement. There were reports coming out of Russia that he had done big property deals with Moscow mafia. John was flying out on his private jet, and selling large-scale timeshare schemes by the block to any businessmen that would listen, it was claimed. He would fly out with a translator and Russian language brochures for the holiday lets.

If the reports were to be believed, gangsters, killers and politicians were investing in the hope that John's businesses could launder their ill-gotten gains. John kept me very much at arm's length from any of this, but it wouldn't be the first time he had been foolish with the company he kept.

On cocaine, John felt invincible. I didn't share his optimism. The newspapers were filled with allegations that his timeshare schemes were bent. One of the first newspaper headlines in 1993 read: 'Victims of a sunshine fraudster: Britons are being bullied and deceived by a timeshare firm in Tenerife'.

The Early Years

John with his brothers at Midge's wedding to Karen in 1983. From left: John, David, Karen, Midge, Mike, and George.

John and Marnie on an early date, Bath, 1974.

John fishing with Marnie in Saltford, near Bath, 1975.

John on fishing trip in Saltford, in the late 1970s.

John at home at Pendennis Rd in 1978.

John and Marnie getting married at Bristol Register Office with their great danes Quincy and Jerry. This picture was featured on front of *Bath Evening Chronicle*.

John and Marnie, with Janie at her christening in Bristol, 1978.

The Tenerife Years

Lunn Poly tourist photo showing John, Marnie and the girls arriving in Tenerife just days before Brink's-Mat police raided their home in Bath.

Picture of the Palmer family at Terry McKay's home in Tenerife, several weeks after they left the hotel.

Press photo taken in the weeks after John was declared a fugitive.

Holidays and Happier Times

John's first plane.

John's second plane – a Jetstream, taken in late '90s at Bristol Airport.

Marnie and her nine-year-old horse, Bambi, at the Coach House in 1999.

John with Sammie at Hyatt Regency, Orlando.

John expresses his delight at finding a £20 note during a meal at the Manor House, Castle Combe, 1995.

John lands his helicopter for lunch at Castle Combe, 1995.

John shooting pigeons with air rifle at Coach House, early 1990s.

Brochure ahead of sale of Coach House, 2013.

THE COACH HOUSE
BATTLEFIELDS
LANSDOWN, BATH, BA1 9DD

DAVID
JAMES
& PARTNERS LLP
Rural Chartered Surveyors
Country House Agents

Marnie and John after catching Wahoo, *c.* 1999.

Marnie with one of
her trained Harris's
Hawk, Oxo. She was
Marnie's first and
favourite.

The Brave Goose off Lanzarote in the mid 1990s.

John and Marnie

John and Marnie.

Waiting to board the plane at Minorca. A classic picture of John with his famous briefcase, phone and book of contacts.

Last holiday at Gleneagles before John was jailed for timeshare fraud.

John and Marnie in Florida, mid 1990s.

Press Photos

Daily Mail picture of the smelting works at the Coach House, *c.* 1985.

Associated Press picture of John and Marnie as fugitives in Tenerife, 1985.

It added:

'The signs on the wall describe it as 'The Ultimate Experience', but for most of the 7,000 timeshare owners of Island Village, Tenerife, even getting in has become the ultimate nightmare. They are the victims of a multi-layered property and cash imbroglio that has cost many of them thousands of pounds more than their original investment and left some with shattered nerves.'

The article said John:

… retains overall control over the 180-villa complex via a complex web of companies in England, the Isle of Man and Tenerife itself.

Lawyers on the island estimate the complex cost the 43-year-old Mr Palmer £6m to build but that his companies have collected tens of millions since.

I confronted John, but he snapped back at me: 'Everyone's doing it. I don't know why it's me who's carrying the can. I've sacked some of my managers for putting too much pressure on. It's me that's getting this under control.'

All I could do was turn my cheek and hope he was able to sort it out.

He was becoming erratic and dangerous to be around, sure-fire signs that he was feeling the strain. The taxman was also chasing him everywhere he went.

It sums up his madness by that stage that he thought drugs were the answer. He said he was doing two grams a day. One close friend said to me: 'If that's what he said, you can double it.'

His biggest drug-demented mistake would lead to humiliation on national television – the 1994 sting by television reporter Roger Cook at the Ritz. *The Cook Report*, an ITV documentary series that carried out investigations on suspected criminals, had been after John for years. I've no idea what John must have done to Cook, but he always had it in for him.

Roger Cook eventually turned over John by asking two stooges to pose as opium growers who needed drugs money 'cleaned'. Secret footage showed John apparently agreeing to the deal, but telling the two Asian heroin dealers: 'I'm not cheap.'

I have since read a quote from Cook saying it was one of his proudest coups to have John offering to launder £100 million on tape. But they had just got lucky by tracking John down when he was high on cocaine. That drug filled his head with the misguided belief that he could say and do as he pleased. He would often talk nonsense, say anything when he was snorting lines.

I remember John phoning me just a few hours before it was on air. He sounded typically cocky about the whole thing.

'Don't worry love – it was all just a joke,' he said. 'I was just winding him up. The joke is on Cook.'

John was wrong. The sting made him look the idiot, especially the moment Cook confronted him on camera at the Ritz and asked him to comment.

'I don't know what you're talking about,' said John, even though the footage clearly showed him offering to launder cash.

John was furious and humiliated by the programme. I knew he was high as soon as I watched his outlandish boast on TV that he offered the best rates in the business for money laundering. He had been such an idiot.

The programme was devastating for me, too. I went to watch it at a friend's as John said I shouldn't be alone. Aside from the allegations of criminality, it was galling to see him in the video describe having sons as well as daughters. He never even talked about the children spawned from his affairs at home, yet here it was, being broadcast on television. I knew my girls would see this, and feel betrayed.

Ultimately, the cocaine binges had got him into this mess. The drug had made him sloppy and careless, traits you would never have associated with John before he got involved with it. For the first time, there was evidence on camera that John was a liar. Ultimately, this would be toxic for his reputation.

I hated that drug, and in those days it was everywhere. In Tenerife and the West Country, it was rife, and probably still is. It made John's nose run, very red and raw around the nostrils. I could tell immediately when he was on it; I think he felt he needed it to stay sharp. It was a vicious circle because the only reason he was losing sleep was because of the drug. He was forever dabbing vapour rub on his nose so he could breathe.

While he knew I hated it, he often tried to make me take it. On the *Goose* he would go on big benders, and try to slip some in my drink. Whenever I threw one of the drinks away, he would rage: 'Don't take yourself so seriously. After all I've done for you.'

That drug made John so arrogant, and it definitely affected his judgement – a sober John would have seen Cook coming. Police told Cook that John paid £20,000 to have him killed. I highly doubt that's true, but John would have been happy he had given him a scare.

The Cook TV fiasco was a huge shot in the arm for Scotland Yard as they busily collected statements from British timeshare investors complaining about the firm's conduct since the early

1990s. Multiple police forces coordinated their attempts to investigate fraud and racketeering claims against John in Britain, across Europe and even Moscow. Officers had already interviewed him in Russia and seized his promotional videos and brochures.

By this stage, Christina was becoming increasingly involved in the business, and was even fronting up for press interviews in John's place. She told *The Independent* the problems were caused by a small minority of timeshare owners.

'It is a few who want things done differently and their tactics stink,' she said.

In public, John laughed it all off. The pressure was nothing like Brink's-Mat, he insisted. But, behind closed doors, the pressure was starting to show. Reality hit home for him when a key member of his team was arrested in 1996. A source then told John the suspect was willing to do a plea bargain and give evidence against him. John was mortified by this betrayal.

He was so shocked he sank into a dark mood and went on a major cocaine binge. He vanished for a weekend. This would end up becoming a regular occurrence, and I suspected there were other women he was seeing, in addition to Christina.

When he returned from that first weekend, he was back to his normal self, insisting there was never any possibility of him being chased by the police. It was a massive change of heart but he had come to the conclusion that nobody on the island would let him get arrested while he was throwing money at them.

John always asserted his innocence, even at home. He maintained that he was a wronged man, accused again and again of crimes he hadn't committed. However, for the first time, it felt like he was no longer in complete control of his business affairs. The timeshare scheme was a juggernaut and other gangs were moving in for a piece of the action. By late 1996, his lieutenant Mohammed Derbah had started out on his own, setting up a rival timeshare firm. This came just a few months after wild newspaper reports alleged Mo was being linked by police to gun smuggling allegations. Of course those claims may have been false, but, eventually, losing Mo was a relief. He had made millions for the company, but John was intimidated by him.

'He's a tricky bastard,' John would say. 'I'm glad to be free of him.'

My husband deserved little sympathy over some of his antics, but many of the people beneath him were even more brutal and ruthless. Without Mo, John had his work cut out keeping his troops in line. He was being watched 24/7 by police and there were huge rows involving his staff. The young sales people would be fired and rehired every week.

The police investigations were not his only concern. By now, his wealth had attracted a lot of enemies, and he was always convinced someone was planning to assassinate him. Officers confirmed his suspicions when they passed on intelligence to him, via an informant, that a contract to kill him was being offered around the underworld. Between 1993 and 1994, the price on his head doubled. Security was stepped up on all the properties and John started keeping a little pistol and some bullets in the cupboard above our bed.

John took a personal bodyguard with him everywhere. There were some horrific stories of violence and gun running circulating. Because he had made such a success of the timeshares, his company was facing the threat of a huge turf war.

The island had changed. Tenerife's rocky southern coastline was now covered with timeshare apartment complexes and beaches made from imported African sand. The barren little settlement of Playas de las Americas was now one of Britain's top tourist destinations. The beaches became saturated with timeshare salesmen as John's rivals tried to get a piece of the pie. Away from the strip, businesses would do whatever they could to survive – even if that meant bloodshed.

John was advised by his security team to keep a low profile. He travelled between his penthouse in the Flamingo Club to another timeshare complex in a beaten up blue Opel Omega. For the first time in life, he didn't want to be recognised on the island. And he definitely didn't want people to see him being flash.

John replaced Mohammed Derbah with Richie, a nice British chap who had worked his way through the ranks. He deserved the chance to be John's number two. John liked the guy, but as the months rolled by I think there were concerns he was using some of the tactics Mo employed. I remember one phone call when we were on the boat. It was 'F•••ing' this, 'F•••ing' that.

'It's out of control, Richie,' he was saying on his mahogany-cased mobile phone. 'They're a fucking liability. They've taken it too far.'

I was getting more and more worked up; the more I found out, the worse it sounded. One day John came back with bruised knuckles. Like always, he came up with a mealy-mouthed cover story, this time saying he fell over. But I wanted to be sure, so I called Richie.

'Marnie, look. I'll be straight with you,' he said. 'You really don't have a clue what John is getting up to over here. That allegation when the woman was hanging from the balcony? That was true. I was there.'

When I confronted John, he just said it was Richie who had held her out of the window. I didn't know who to believe. At that point, I trusted neither of them.

It was a stressful time and John fought the public relations war like he had with Brink's-Mat, giving several interviews to the press. He told the *Bristol Evening Post* through his London solicitor, Henry Milner, that he had not been involved with Island Village for six years and had no links with the management company. Unfortunately, this version of events was undermined by the paperwork for the business that confirmed it was still registered in his name.

John sold the Island Village complex soon after it was completed, to seventeen separate companies, known as Island Village Units Numbers One to Seventeen, registered in Ramsey, Isle of Man. But his own Island Village Management Ltd, registered in Douglas, Isle of Man, continued to market the timeshares.

Then, just when he needed them least, the Brink's-Mat insurers came back to retrieve more of his profits. His legal team was informed he was subject to an asset-freezing Mareva Injunction gained from the High Court of Justice, enabling investigators to track his substantial financial resources.

John was in and out of legal meetings all day. As well as the Brink's-Mat civil claims, the timeshare complaints were piling up. At one point it seemed everyone around him was baying for blood. The entire business was in chaos.

My husband would come to the boat upset and on edge. I would hear him on the phone raging at his staff: 'What have you done? This is getting out of control.'

But whenever I asked, I just heard 'don't worry', 'relax love', 'it's fine'.

I tried to believe him. Brink's-Mat seemed a lifetime ago and I hoped John was becoming too powerful for police to touch. But there was so much bad news in the papers about my husband. You would have needed your head in the clouds to feel confident about the future.

*

In the autumn of 1996 – nine years after John swaggered out of the Old Bailey a free man – police swooped again to arrest him. After their Brink's-Mat embarrassment, Scotland Yard had another chance to claw back some pride.

We had flown from Barbados on Concorde into Heathrow Airport. John was approached and taken away by two officers as he stood in the queue for customs. I didn't know what was going on.

In a panic, I got all the bags together and took the girls back in the Range Rover. We turned the wrong way, towards London, and got lost. When we eventually got on the M4, a convoy of police cars with their blue lights flashing came speeding past us. In the middle vehicle, John was in the back seat, waving and smiling at us. He clearly found the whole thing hilarious. I was simply amazed they thought they needed three cars to keep my little old husband in check!

John was questioned about a host of different offences. It came as a huge shock to me that detectives believed John had helped Noye escape the country in May after the stabbing of Stephen Cameron. The offence sounded horrible, and pretty typical of a renowned hothead like Noye. The road rage attack took place in broad daylight at the Swanley interchange of the M25 in Kent. Within minutes of the attack, Noye had fled the country, carrying a briefcase full of cash. Noye was still on the run, but police had been monitoring Noye's mobile phone and reckoned John helped fly him out by helicopter to France and then by private jet to Madrid.

The Noye link was the hook to arrest him, but they also wanted to quiz John about the timeshare claims.

When I got the girls home to Bath, police were everywhere, turning the place upside down. They had even set the burglar alarms off at the neighbouring Chapel Cottage. It was chaos. The police asked me to turn the alarms off, but I refused.

'They're called intruder alarms for a reason,' I said, resolutely.

Those alarms were making a deafening racket. We ended up getting complaints from the neighbours, but it was my one way of protesting against all this ridiculous heavy-handed treatment.

We had a housekeeper at the time who, unbeknown to us, was training to be a barrister. She was so mortified by the whole thing that she did a runner. When I eventually got hold of her, she said her career might be in tatters.

As I walked around my home with the alarms blaring, a policewoman followed me everywhere. She then led me into my youngest daughter's bedroom where officers were rifling through the drawers. I flipped my lid.

'What are you doing? She's just a child,' I shrieked. 'What do you want?'

The young policewoman replied: 'John's been a naughty boy, and some people hide drugs in their children's rooms.'

She then added: 'What can you tell us about John and Kenneth Noye?'

John swore until he was blue in the face that he had never met the bloke. They laid eyes on each other just once in his entire life, when John went to see his solicitor in London.

'John knows absolutely nothing about this,' I told police. Still to this day, I believe he had nothing to do with helping him. Detectives finally tracked Noye down two years later and he was convicted of murder in 2000.

John was eventually bailed without charge, but he knew the police would be chasing him relentlessly over the coming months. It was now only a matter of time before they made a move over the timeshares. They also claimed to suspect him of gun and drug trafficking.

Officers came again to the Coach House a few months later, claiming they were looking for paperwork and drugs. Instead, they eventually found guns and one pistol in the neighbouring cottage where John had his office.

Officers took me over to the cottage, and I couldn't believe my eyes. One of them pulled out a deadly stun gun and showed it to me. 'What are you keeping this for?' he asked.

I had no answer for him. John banned me from going into that cottage, unless I was bringing him over tea and biscuits for his business meetings. He said the weapons were only there for shooting rabbits, and lamping on the estate – but I'm not sure that explanation would wash given that we didn't have any licences.

To my horror, they arrested me in connection with the pistol. I was very worried and they had me at Bridewell Police Station in central Bristol for hours before John's London solicitor came down the M4 and got me bail. Clearly it wasn't anything to do with me, but probably because I was so difficult and obstructive, I ended up getting charged.

I then had to go back to Bridewell just before Christmas. I worried they were going to lock me up, but John found it funny. I was being prosecuted for being armed without a licence, even though it was nothing to do with me. I was furious with John.

'They're only after me,' he said. 'Their case will collapse against you – it won't be worth the hassle.'

As I left the station, I remember the police officer smirking and saying, 'Have a nice Christmas.'

I just growled back at him. I was worried to death about being locked up, and leaving my two daughters.

However, John was right about my gun charge; the prosecution was eventually dropped the following March. I could have been jailed, but police had bigger fish to fry than a minnow like me. John would be the prize catch.

Despite the gun charge being dropped, I was depressed. It didn't help that, a few months later in 1997, I had to give up horse riding.

I had a terrible bout of salmonella that left me bedridden. Eventually I was taken to hospital, where I developed septic arthritis. My joints swelled up. For weeks, I couldn't even stand up. By the time I got on a horse again, I felt very uncomfortable. My knees and back were just too painful to let me relax. I felt very unstable, and lost my nerve. It may seem silly, but it was a real blow to me. The horses were my passion. Without them, there was no release valve for the stress.

I also struggled to get out to the boat for several months. There was a lot of time to mull over my life with John. I was fast coming to my senses about John's lying – there was so much that he had been hiding from me. For the first time, I realised that it was the beginning of the end of our marriage.

It was galling to learn his cheating wasn't limited to Christina. There was another long-term affair and love child with a statuesque German student, Saskia Mundinger. I first heard from Saskia in the early 1990s, at least five years after they began their tawdry liaisons. Saskia phoned me to say John had been refusing to pay any money for their toddler son, Parish. I was ex-directory but she said she had found me after searching through John's little phone book. John, of course, would continue to deny everything, but over the next four years, the evidence started piling up, most notably legal demands for maintenance from Saskia's solicitor. By the mid-90s I knew he was cheating. It was devastating.

I became convinced there were more grubby secrets that John was keeping from me. I could no longer live in a bubble, ignoring the truth. By 1997, I wanted a divorce.

11

OTHER WOMEN

'Unpredictable, volatile and frightening' – my solicitor repeated that phrase in three divorce petitions we sent to John. In the black and white of legal print, our forty-year marriage read like a Hammer horror script.

However, looking back now, this was a crass assessment. The truth, like so often in life, was a good deal more confusing. John could be wonderful company, the most welcoming man you could meet. He loved a joke, a meal out with friends, and he could be extremely generous. John was magnetic, charming and there was an enduring love between us. What destroyed us was his drug-taking, womanising and violence. Our marriage veered from exciting and loving to, on any given day, deceitful, angry and terrifying.

To explain the full extent of his cheating, I will need to go back to the beginning. I feel as though I have lived two lives: one where I was aware of the affairs, and the other when I pretended I could live in blissful ignorance.

I now know the affairs lasted from the early days of our marriage until the day he died. Janie was still a toddler in

1979 when the clues started piling up that he had a long-term mistress.

John was running his jewellery business across the West Country then and, for the first time in his life, he had started wearing suits. I hoped this was a sign he was working in other worlds, really starting to care about his appearance to impress clients. But then, like a low-budget melodrama, I spotted a lipstick mark on his white shirt. Then he stopped wearing his wedding ring, claiming it was uncomfortable. At the time, my mother was working at one of his shops in Bath, and she had heard he was openly carousing with a shop assistant. Clearly there was a pattern of behaviour forming even then, but John just laughed this off when I confronted him. He knew I was powerless, with a young baby to look after.

Perhaps I should have cut my losses early on? I hope you can believe me that this was not a choice of money over morals. My greatest fear for at least a decade was that he would take our girls to Tenerife and I would never see them again. I had heard of jilted husbands taking their children overseas before with a lot less money than John had. His team of lawyers would have run rings around me. And if that didn't work, perhaps he could have had me finished off.

Then, as his power, influence and notoriety grew, my voice in our relationship dwindled. For years, I hoped he would give up the women and come back to me, even as the warning signs blared through me like a faulty fire alarm. Maybe I deserve no sympathy. Misguided or not, the betrayals left me with a sense of guilt, and a deep sense of sadness.

I thought perhaps it was my fault for not satisfying his desires. John would often make sexual suggestions that shocked me. He had told me he wanted a threesome. He had visions of a woman on either side in bed with him. He said he knew a woman in London who would be keen. I was just too traditional for that sort of thing. It didn't appeal to me at all. I have suspicions he was seeing prostitutes, too.

Then there are the two long-term significant others. For years I had believed Saskia and Christina were the same person. There was the 'Goldfinger's Lover' front page on the paper after the Brink's-Mat trial. For years, I thought that was Christina, as I couldn't bear to actually read the article. But then BBC coverage years later would show a completely different woman depicted as 'Christina'.

'That can't be Christina,' I shouted at the television. But, of course, it was; it had been my mistake all those years before. In fact, the woman on that front page in 1987 was Saskia. She confirmed this to me over the phone during her desperate attempts to get maintenance money from John in the mid-90s.

'We have been seeing each other for years,' she said on the phone. To prove her point she read out the details of recent flights John had paid for.

'He flew me backwards and forwards to Jersey where we spent the night. He also took me to Sardinia from Strasbourg, where I live.'

To my horror, they were going away for stolen weekends in hotels across Europe, usually locking themselves away in their room because they were both taking cocaine. Saskia claimed John made her take it.

I was so shocked by this I had to see a doctor. Saskia eventually took John to court over support payments for their son, Parish. It was eventually agreed that he would set up a trust fund for his son, which would be released when he was 18.

It beggars belief to think John spent three decades dividing his time between three women, constantly filling our heads with lies.

For John, it was the more the merrier. He had an insatiable appetite for sex, more than one woman would want.

Both the affairs stretched back to the very start of John's business interests in Tenerife. Christina had been an assistant for John, while Saskia would eventually work in the sales team, having met John on the island while she was still a student.

I later found out that the pair of them had been visiting weekly at HMP Brixton, on separate days from me. I had listened to all John's sob stories as I visited him twice a week without fail. I brought him roasts, spaghetti bolognese, his ironing and magazines every week, trudging up that hill from the station with the girls. We would set off at 6.30 a.m. Yet, after all this effort, I was just filling in the gaps between his other women. It broke my heart that they both bore him sons. What a mug he had made of me.

John saw Christina for her brain and Saskia out of lust. Saskia drove him spare with her demands, but he found her irresistible. 'Saskia's a money-grabbing bitch,' he screamed at me once.

In 1993, we went on holiday to Barbados and he was constantly upstairs talking on the phone to her. He would sneak upstairs, but I could hear him whispering through the door. He was telling her he was away in rehab, trying to kick his crippling drug habit. Clearly, there was no way he would ever have gone to a clinic. Too proud, too macho. Even behind my back he couldn't be honest. He just lied and lied until he was blue in the face.

One of John's close friends tried to reassure me that he was trying to get rid of Saskia, but this was small comfort. These secret phone conversations sparked one hell of a row between us. The next day the manager of the five-star Caribbean hotel where we were staying told us we would have to leave if this carried on. Neither of us cared though; our marriage had become a volcano with daily eruptions.

Saskia sparked the worst scenes between us; John certainly had his hands full keeping her happy. Shortly after we returned to Bath, I had a phone call and it was a German-sounding woman. I knew who it was, long before she introduced herself.

'We have a son together and we are very much in love,' said this shrill, annoying voice. Before I could get a word in, she added: 'John was there at his birth and he takes me everywhere. He has bought me diamonds, fur coats, a bungalow, a piano and sends planes to pick me up. John loves my body so much that sometimes he cries after sex because he doesn't believe I enjoy it as much as him.'

I stood open-mouthed in the kitchen of the Coach House as she said that he had told her he was leaving me. He had furnished her home, bought her hundreds of thousands of pounds of jewellery and fur coats.

What do you say to that? I just hung up. It had hit me like a sledgehammer but John, like he so often did, just laughed it off. 'It's just a load of rubbish,' he said. 'Just forget about it. She's just after my money.'

They were a terrible influence on each other.

I warned John I would divorce him if he cheated again, but I shouldn't have bothered. He carried on nipping off for sordid encounters with her, even when we were on holiday together. There was always a different excuse. For years, I didn't have a clue. John even managed to creep off for sex when we took our horse over to Verden, Germany, to compete.

'I love it round here – I'm just going for a drive,' he told me one morning as I was heading to the stables near our hotel.

In fact, he was driving a 200-mile round trip for sex at Saskia's apartment. She told me this over the phone about six months later. I felt sick, but I had to hand it to him. His attitude to cheating on me was much like his business approach – he would go to almost any lengths to seal the deal!

It continued for years. In 1998, John told us on Boxing Day at Gleneagles that he was flying off for a few days on the Isle of Skye. 'It's my dream, love. I want to stay in a log cabin and enjoy complete solitude, get away from it all. Do you mind if I leave you with the girls for a few days?'

He had only joined us two days earlier, but, of course, I accepted he probably needed a break from the ongoing police investigation. A few weeks later, I was back at the Coach House when I found out the truth: he had flown off to meet Saskia in a bid to keep her sweet.

Saskia told me by phone how she had been hammering on our door in Bath that Christmas Day as John hadn't sent any money for their son. When he was nowhere to be found, she filed a report to Avon and Somerset Police at Bridewell Police Station. Clearly John had committed no crime relating to Saskia, but detectives were more than happy to talk to this distressed woman, with make-up running down her face.

She told police all her sordid secrets about her life with John, but knew nothing of any note about his business. She asked the police to help pressure John to pay maintenance, but, of course, there was nothing they could do. Then she drove down to Christina's house in Essex to confront her instead.

Again John denied Saskia's version of events, but, of course, I couldn't believe a word of it. You really never knew where the truth started and the lie finished with John.

'I will never forgive him,' Saskia had told me. 'While I was pregnant, he would tell me to take cocaine. I ran out of the hotel room but his bodyguards forced me back in. He is out of control. He is an abuser, and he doesn't care about you either.'

Fortunately their son, Parish, was healthy despite this. Saskia's parents would help with childcare, and she was able to start over again. I would grow to envy them.

I was the opposite. I was in limbo. John had taken all my strength, and I was stuck with him. Lonely, with no self-respect, I filled my life with caring for my daughters and horses. I did what I thought I should do, but probably what I needed was to cut my ties and leave John.

It could all have been so different. In 1987, while John was awaiting trial for Brink's-Mat, I considered leaving him for another man. It all started when my mum and stepdad came up to live with me at the Coach House while he was on remand. They knew how stressed I was and encouraged me to go out for the night, agreeing to look after my two girls. I met an old friend in Swindon who introduced me to a pal of his. We got on straight away. The interest was flattering. There were no illicit nights of passion with this new man, but we did exchange cards, and eventually long letters. Before long, we were baring our souls. I felt like I was falling in love again.

Then my mum rummaged through my handbag and found some of these notes. She went crazy. 'You're going to give up all this?' she shouted, looking around at the Coach House. 'And your daughters, what about them?'

We had a terrible row. Eventually, my mum and dad packed up and left. My eldest daughter was also desperately upset, and couldn't understand what was happening.

Then, behind my back, my mother went to see John in prison, and told him all about this 'affair' and that she was worried I was planning to leave him. She even told John I was an 'unfit mother', and said if he would give her £100 a week, she would take care of the girls.

As usual, you had to expect the unexpected with John. Instead of being angry with me, he turned his rage on mum. Glaring at mum across the table at Brixton, John yelled: 'How can you go behind your own daughter's back like this? Do you think this is something I need to hear, while I'm locked up twenty-four hours a day? What does this achieve? I think it's disgusting you would do this.'

I was amazed when my dad eventually relayed this back to me. But it was typical John. He could be evil to me, but if anyone else tried to cross me, they would get it much worse. Perhaps, in his own way, this was showing a bit of loyalty. You keep your issues behind closed doors.

However, John believed my indiscretion gave him carte blanche to see or do whatever he liked. After his release, you never knew where you were with him. He was charm personified one minute, then ice cold the next.

To keep me sweet he showered me with gifts. I loved having horses, and I ended up with five. I poured all my love into them and the children. The horses were such an escape from John's twisted mind games.

But worse was to come as the drugs eroded his self-control. Fits of rage turned into physical attacks. The worst one of all took place after I decided to get myself sterilised.

It was an attack that came from nowhere. Having come to the decision that I couldn't have another child with John, he didn't seem bothered. The night after the operation, he even took me for a meal. As we sat together, his warmth and charm reassured me. It had been such a vulnerable, raw time. John was warm and caring over dinner. I thought the realisation that we would have no more children might have been the shock he needed. Perhaps it was almost a relief.

Of course, I could not have been more wrong. When we got home, I couldn't remember the alarm code. John hit the roof. He punched me in the face, with his phone still in his hand, and then pushed me to the ground and kicked me. I gasped in pain and could barely take a breath. I remember opening my eyes through the tears to see my oldest daughter staring back at me. She was transfixed, frozen in fear. The look on her face still gives me nightmares. That was the moment I realised I had deluded myself about any hope that our marriage could recover.

John spent the night with a friend after that. The next morning I went to speak to a lawyer in Chippenham about divorce options. I was so unsure what to do. I was convinced John would take the girls from me. The lawyer was very encouraging about the case. 'You have very good grounds for a sizeable settlement,' he said, 'The violence against you is unacceptable. You need to go after him.'

A fortnight later John launched into another rage after I confronted him over Christina. He battered me in the Range Rover with his car phone, which was the size of a small brick in those days. It had a polished wood finish. The blow was so hard that my doctor said nerves had been damaged in my face.

The crazed fits of temper were a weekly occurance by this stage. There was one time he was pestering me to take cocaine with him on the boat. I kept refusing and it bruised his ego so much that he stormed off ashore for two days. When he came back, he punched me across the jaw with the force of a heavyweight boxer. There was blood everywhere. Enough.

I went to a solicitor again to formally launch divorce proceedings. We discussed my situation for hours. I see now that the case must have been this lawyer's dream ticket. Evidence of drugs, violence and criminality; my young solicitor was relishing his day in court. He thought he could get stuck into a massive divorce settlement, and probably earn himself a nice slice of John's fortune. It was obvious John would cut off financial support, but the lawyer immediately told me that I would be in a strong position, and my husband would be ordered to sell off his assets to give me a chunk of what was rightly mine.

He wrote up a blistering attack on John. Looking at the letter now, it still shocks me. It was the payoff line in the divorce file that really summed it up: 'Throughout the marriage, the respondent's behaviour and moods have been unpredictable, volatile and frightening. The respondent would go into a rage unreasonably and be extremely frightening and domineering, much to the petitioner's humiliation, anxiety and distress.'

John got the letter in June 1998 but, typically for him, he wouldn't sign the agreement. He was a control freak about everything. And an arch dealmaker. He certainly wasn't going to accept a divorce that wasn't on his own terms. Also, I think a part of him wanted to save the marriage. Despite all the horrors, there was still love between us, albeit a bit twisted. It was very confusing. He was still spending a huge amount of money trying to keep me and the girls happy. During one row he defended one of his attacks by shouting, 'But you liked the money.' To some extent, he was right. I had seen the world and enjoyed the financial freedoms. The money gave me the chance to look after our girls – and, most importantly, ensure they couldn't be taken away from me.

With his drug-addled mood swings to contend with, his firearms filled me with terror. He was so unpredictable. I particularly hated that gun being in the cupboard above our head in the bedroom. It felt so inevitable that it was only a matter of time before the barrel was pointed at me. The horror

began when I was sent a newspaper article about John. I forget
the paper; it was the *Sun* or *Mirror*. Alongside the piece was a
picture captioned 'Marnie', but it wasn't me. It was another
blonde woman with a little boy. Christina, Saskia and now
her. Another son, too? John had always wanted boys. I broke
down in tears and ran into our bedroom screaming at John,
who was still in bed.

'How many others?' I screeched. 'Who else have you had
babies with? I'm leaving.'

As I ran at him, he whipped the pistol from under his
pillow, and pointed it straight into the side of my head. I was
convinced he was going to kill me. Time slowed down as he
pulled the trigger. 'Die, you bitch,' John shouted, then cackled:
'Not loaded, see.'

I collapsed on the bed, crying and heartbroken. John just
yelled at me, 'Get out, get out.' Still, to this day, I do not know
who that third woman was.

12

TIME'S UP

In the end the police got to John before my lawyers were able to get their claws in over a divorce case. Detectives charged him over a staggeringly long list of timeshare fraud allegations after he decided to fly back to the UK to hand himself in.

In theory, John had enough money to stay in Tenerife for the rest of his years, paying off every detective that came sniffing around. But the Met Police's campaign to net him – stretching all the way back to the Brink's-Mat investigation – had ground him down. He was under twenty-four-hour surveillance, all his properties were bugged and he was wracked with paranoia. John's problem wasn't only that Spanish police, Russian authorities and Scotland Yard were sharpening their knives. Countless underworld enemies were queuing up for his blood because he had made such a huge amount of money.

At the front of the line, he believed, were associates of those that had either died or been jailed as a result of the Brink's-Mat raid. There was a huge amount of envy and jealousy at John's situation. He was the only one who had apparently come out of it all both free and unscathed. There were rumours of the 'Brink's-Mat curse' looming over those that had been involved. The press noticed that a string of murders had befallen men with links to the bullion. As much as 70 per cent of the haul has never been traced, and bitter disputes were still rumbling over the rightful owners of the spoils.

The papers made for grim reading: Great Train Robber Charlie Wilson was gunned down at his Marbella home after £3 million of Brink's-Mat money apparently went missing in a drug deal. Then, in 1996, Keith Hedley, a suspected money launderer, was shot dead by three men on his yacht off the coast of Corfu. Two years later, Hatton Garden jeweller Solly Nahome, who had helped move hundreds of gold bars, was also shot dead outside his home. Brian Perry, who was jailed for handling gold, died after being shot three times in the head in south London at the age of 63 following his release in 2001. The same year, Brink's-Mat gang member George Francis, 63, was gunned down at point-blank range in his car outside the courier business he ran in south-east London.

John was hardly surprised when the Met Police told him a price had been put out in the underworld for his assassination. The pressure was building from every angle, and he was losing control.

We were sailing on the *Brave Goose* when he decided it was all too much. Unlike the Brink's-Mat, John did understand deep down that he had a case to answer over the timeshare fraud. It was a beautiful sunny afternoon. John turned to me and said: 'The pressure is getting too much. The police are everywhere.'

Since stepping up their investigation into John's financial activities in 1994, police had turned up the heat to boiling point. The pressure was immense, and he felt giving himself up was the only way to buy himself good favour with the jury.

'At least if I hand myself in, it will be on my terms. I can take control.'

That was everything for John; he always had to be the one holding the cards. People speculated that he would offer a deal, passing information for a lighter sentence. But that wasn't John at all. Despite handing himself in, he would still go down fighting.

'I'm going to fly back to Britain,' he said. 'Don't worry, I just need to sort this out.' That was the last time we shared the bedroom together on our beloved boat. I would return to the Coach House, still as his wife and still in the marital bedroom, until his dying day. But nothing would ever be the same again.

He reported himself to Spanish police and then flew to Britain in his private jet. The timing was fortunate as we were later told police had been poised to arrest him anyway. Officers made it clear to him they had been burned over Brink's-Mat. They were not going to let a second chance at locking him up slip by.

For Scotland Yard police chiefs, their lucky day had arrived. John Palmer in cuffs, and they hadn't even needed to break sweat. John was weak, too; a shadow of his former self thanks to the drugs and stress.

'I'll be fine,' he told me on the phone after securing £1 million bail. But this would be nothing like the previous trial; this time the case against him was immense.

On 11 April 1997, he made a preliminary appearance in court charged with eight counts of timeshare fraud worth £15 million. John handed the Clerkenwell magistrate a £1 million banker's draft for bail. Amazingly, his bail restrictions allowed him to travel overseas. He was ushered away from the court by three minders, who helped him into a Range Rover with blacked out windows. By the next morning, he was on a plane back to Tenerife.

John would continue with business as normal as he waited to face trial, but the situation on the ground in Tenerife became even more dangerous. Violence repeatedly erupted in Playas de las Americas. John's bars, hotels and clubs were all prime targets for criminal gangs.

John was still on bail in July 1999 when Mohammed Derbah and his brother, Hassan, were badly beaten up. They were set upon by a gang of six Britons wielding baseball bats. The Spanish authorities say the six had been contracted as security guards by another company to police the activities of their own timeshare touts and prevent them being poached by competitors.

Spanish police tried to link the attacks on Mohammed and his brother with John. Officers said the attack was part of a 'bitter struggle', a turf war between rivals.

But the last thing my husband wanted was more bother. He was no longer the man with the Midas touch on that island, and there was no point in getting involved in violence. His reputation was now taking a battering on the Canaries and across Spain. Tenerife police were facing increased international scrutiny and were now making dozens of arrests a week connected with fraud, violence and racketeering.

Officers investigating the case told the press: 'It's an extremely competitive world, with huge commercial interests at play. A young timeshare salesman can earn up to a million pesetas [£4,000] a day. Imagine the money the company makes. The role of the salesman is crucial. It's a closed world even to the security forces, it organises itself and largely polices itself, so that complaints are rarely made public. There is a bitter struggle between timeshare companies that lies behind this latest violence.' In response, John gave an ill-advised interview to *The Independent* newspaper. His intention in agreeing to meet the journalist was to settle a few scores, pointing out some of the corruption he had seen among police ranks.

However, the journalist, Elizabeth Nash, didn't swallow this story. Instead, she slaughtered him.

John insisted to Nash that he wasn't worried at all about his trial. 'Why should I worry, Elizabeth? I won't be sent down. I'll take as long as it takes to prove that I'm totally innocent. There's not one thing I'm worried about. Only a guilty person is worried.'

But Nash wasn't impressed with his act of bravado, and she hung him out to dry with his own quotes, depicting him as a paranoid wreck.

She quoted him in full as he asked, 'Why are you here, Elizabeth? What do you want from this interview? I don't like talking to the press. I don't want this taped. It's just a briefing. I'll tape it then give you the tape. You just take notes.'

She then wrote, 'In his flat Brummy tones he launches into tidal waves of detail, repetition and vehement persuasion. I must have looked perplexed.'

John said:

I'm trying to put into your head, Elizabeth, why I'm being persecuted. They tried to get me for money laundering and failed. They couldn't get into the Spanish accounts. They spent seven months in the Isle of Man. Nothing. I made millions in timeshare. There's a few silly complaints about timeshares that were to be resold by four companies. So they said, let's slap that on him. They said I'd defrauded people who wanted to resell timeshares. But I was hardly here.

John, sitting alongside Ramon, his Spanish lawyer, explained that many of the charges against him took place when he was learning to pilot planes and helicopters.

'That was the time I was not involved,' John said. 'I was burnt out, in semi-retirement, and took up a lifetime's ambition of flying big commercial helicopters. I qualified to pilot three types of helicopters.'

John stumbled on his words as Elizabeth asked the obvious question: 'But what about the complaints to the press by people saying that they'd lost money?'

He could only reply: 'What reports?'

To that response, she passed across the table a pile of newspaper clippings. 'We didn't have that many complaints in fifteen years, did we, Ramon, maybe a hundred or so? Not a big deal.'

He said allegations that customers were frogmarched to banks were 'rubbish':

Maybe there was one client who got drunk and got into a fight with a security guard. You know Spain, do you think anyone can march anyone to a bank without them complaining to the police? I don't walk around threatening anyone.

The explanation clearly didn't convince this reporter. John told Nash to look instead at police corruption. 'The real story is the total police corruption and using millions of pounds of public funds – for what, Elizabeth? Chartered accountants say I've lost £10 million.'

Then came a quote that sums up the way John felt about everything: 'I'm no angel, but I'm no gangster. I've become a silly gangster legend ... I don't know why ... They blame me for everything.'

The whole interview was a naive move on John's part. Why would a newspaper be interested in printing his sob story?

John was mad to think Elizabeth was going to write up this story the way he was suggesting. It was indicative of his arrogance at the time. When the interview finally crashed to a halt, John refused to hand over her dictaphone.

Inevitably he was furious about the interview when it appeared in print, but I told him he only had himself to blame. 'This is what happens when you surround yourself with yes men. They encourage you to do the most stupid things.'

★

Just weeks before that national newspaper humbling, John made his most ridiculous decision of all: representing himself in court. The months before the trial were mayhem as John sacked his legal team. They had enraged him by daring to suggest he might want to plead guilty. He just wouldn't listen to anyone.

John based himself with Christina in Essex and attempted to digest one of the most complex fraud cases of all time. There were rooms full of files and documents. Despite his limited literacy skills, he would have to understand everything and then formulate a robust enough defence to convince a jury of his innocence. Of course, this was completely impossible, but John had such belief in himself after his performance in the witness box when he was called to give evidence in the Brink's-Mat trial. He grew convinced he was innocent again. In his mind, he would prove to the jury that his staff may have stepped out of line, but it wasn't under his orders. He thought he could charm the jury all over again.

John and Christina would be tried together on charges of allegedly swindling thousands of British holidaymakers, mostly pensioners, out of their savings. John's 31-year-old nephew, Andrew Palmer, would also face trial.

The three of them were encouraged when the first trial was abandoned over a legal row, but the judge eventually pressed ahead in the autumn of 2000 at the Old Bailey.

With Christina in the dock, I couldn't bear to be there. Though I knew all about her by this point, we had never been in each other's company. The thought of seeing her alongside John in court was just too much humiliation to take.

Instead, I relied on reports and conversations with John to keep abreast of everything. Given his notoriety, I expected it to be wall-to-wall news coverage. Yet there were just one or two reporters who decided to cover the case throughout. The only reporter to file regular in-depth dispatches was Paul Cheston of the *London Evening Standard*. I had to get the paper sent down to Bath every day to keep up with it all. I think other reporters were initially put off by the fact it was such a complex fraud case.

As it turned out, they missed a blockbuster act. John, in his pinstripe suit, puffed out his chest and launched into the most extraordinary defence of his own case. 'I have been portrayed as a gangster,' John told the jury on the first day of the trial. 'I am not a gangster or ever have been a gangster.'

Court 12 is always reserved for the most complicated, time-consuming cases of fraud, but few in history would match this one; it went on for almost a year. At the Bailey, the suspects on trial are normally forced to sit in the dock, surrounded by glass and wood. John, however, was never one for the cheap seats, and he revelled in his place on the front bench surrounded by six bewigged and gowned barristers, including two QCs.

John, Christina and Andrew all denied two charges of conspiracy to defraud between 1989 and 1997. However, Scotland Yard told the court the three of them had effectively conned more than 16,500 victims into buying holiday homes on

Tenerife. The alleged targets included retired police officers, war heroes and even a former trading standards officer. John had netted anything up to £30 million via thirteen Tenerife resorts, prosecutors claimed.

The Crown claimed John ran a sophisticated web of companies based in Brentwood, Essex, which operated a two-pronged sting. With the first prong, dubbed 'buy-sell', existing timeshare owners would be sweet-talked into signing up for weeks at a new holiday home on the basis that their other weeks would be sold for a huge profit. With the second, known as 'rental', new holidaymakers were convinced the timeshare they were buying would be rented out, virtually paying for itself.

It was a 'slick, well-orchestrated and thoroughly dishonest' operation, prosecutor David Farrer QC told the jury. 'Customers were faced with complex, misleading paperwork and a confusing network of companies. These companies pretended to be independent of each other, but the companies were all, in truth, controlled by one man – John Palmer.'

All the victims tempted with the promise of a quick profit were left with nothing except contractual exposure to massive debts, the court heard. However, John fired back at the charges, claiming he was a target of police corruption. He said he was a legitimate businessman who had never taken part in any fraud. He also told the jury all about his past involvement in Brink's-Mat because, he said, the police were resentful of his not guilty verdict and corruptly lined their pockets with reward money from loss adjusters.

John told the court: 'They have done anything to try and get me, and have spent millions and millions of pounds of public money to get me. I am not guilty, nor is Miss Ketley and nor is Andrew Palmer.'

I was horrified by the accounts of timeshare investors who had lost their life savings.

John was shocked to see a number of former clients march in and out of the witness box to describe their ordeals. Bernard Mumby from Pudsey, West Yorkshire, reportedly told how he and his wife lost £5,000, were forced to take out a bank loan, and spent five years in debt. They had been holidaying in Tenerife in 1993 when Bernard was approached by a tout selling scratchcards, who told them they had won a substantial prize. 'He took us to a complex and wanted to sell us timeshare at club La Paz,' said Mr Mumby.

The Mumbys had no interest because they already owned a similar apartment in northern Tenerife, but the salesman said they could sell that one in a few months for £5,000 compared with the £3,500 they had paid for it, and if not they would get their money back. They went through with the deal and when nothing happened they returned to Tenerife in September 1995 to confront sales staff.

'I said I thought we had been told lies,' said Mr Mumby. But he claimed a member of John's team brushed off the claim with a shrug: 'Well, that's good salesmanship.'

Meanwhile, York pensioners John Davidson and wife Vera said they were offered £19,500 for their existing two-week timeshare if they bought a week at the Yuka Park resort. They paid a deposit and £4,200 in monthly instalments, but the original weeks were never sold and when they stopped paying for the extra week it was taken back.

When they complained, they were told all the papers had been sent to head office and then a salesman said bluntly: 'You're not the kind of people we want here.' In the end the couple had to dispose of their original two weeks themselves for just £1,500 each.

Ruth Parsons, of Highgate, told the jury how she and her husband were visiting Playas de las Americas in May 1995 when they were stopped by a tout and, after any number of offers involving their existing timeshares, were escorted to a bank to withdraw £2,000 and hand over a deposit for a new one.

The evidence was pretty damning, even from my point of view. Fortunately John was able to placate at least one alleged victim.

Grandfather Roy Reeve, from Norwich, told how he and his wife had lost £8,000 trying to treat his young granddaughter to a holiday in Tenerife to help her recover from a serious riding accident. John rose to his feet and asked the witness: 'After the last trial, did you receive a cheque from me?'

Reeve: 'Yes I did, thank you.'

John: 'Not at all. That was the first opportunity I had.'

Next up giving evidence was a police officer John was very familiar with – former Scotland Yard commander Roy Ramm. John was angry but not a bit surprised as Ramm described him as 'a serious organised criminal'. In return, John accused Ramm and his colleagues of corruption, while the former police chief cited the allegations made in the Roger Cook programme. Ramm had been a thorn in John's side for years. The pair hated each other.

'Our view was that you were a serious organised criminal trapped by his own words into admitting laundering money,' Ramm said, adding that he had considered this evidence of money laundering but it was decided instead to prosecute John on the timeshare charges.

The next day, former Detective Sergeant Tony Curtis really got John's back up by calling him a liar. Time after time, Judge Gerald Gordon glowered over his bifocals and wearily ordered John to 'get back to the point'.

John threatened to bring 'my lawyers down here' to sue Mr Curtis. 'No, you won't do that, Mr Palmer,' intervened the judge. I said to John afterwards: 'You would have been better off bringing your lawyers down for the bloody trial, not just to sue a cop.'

The jury, it seemed, were loving the spectacle. *Evening Standard* court correspondent Cheston would later write: 'I have never seen a jury enjoy a fraud trial more – in fact I have never seen them enjoy one at all. The seven men and five women are all transfixed, leaning forward, weighing up each witness and wondering what Palmer will do next.'

John's defence was complicated. He alleged detectives were using bogus warrants to search his premises and bank accounts and illegally pass on evidence to the loss adjusters for Brink's-Mat.

In response, solicitor Robert McConn, instructed by the loss adjusters on the Brink's-Mat case, claimed contact with the police was inevitable and above board. He told of the years spent tracking down those involved in the gold robbery and all others who came into contact with the bullion in order to sue them in the civil courts to recover the money.

In the end, fifty-four civil writs were issued against all sorts of defendants, including well-known banks that had unwittingly handled the money and John himself, who, the previous jury had decided, had also been involved innocently.

McConn then detailed for the first time exactly how much had been retrieved from the lost gold. He went on to say that the loss adjusters' lawyers – independent of the police – had made inquiries about John's bank accounts in the UK, Tenerife and the Isle of Man before he struck an out-of-court deal on confidential terms. By the end of the £9 million investigation across eleven countries,

Mr McConn and his colleagues had recovered around £20 million of the £26 million stolen. But, as John pointed out, if the proceeds had been invested, it would have been worth £70 million to £80 million by then.

'So you only got back about a third ... still, you done well,' said John. 'But you didn't know how rich I am. You could have sued me for £50 million,' he went on. 'Were you aware of my private plane? (pause) And my two helicopters (laughter from the jury which Palmer waits to subside) ... and I've got one or two cars (even more laughter).'

In a bid to explain away the timeshare victims' complaints, John told the jury how problems arose after he took on sales director Brendan Hannon, who had been working for a rival company. Hannon brought in his own 'dream team', John claimed, and the fraud took place behind his back as he had been too busy learning to fly his Learjet and helicopter.

After nine months, the jury finally retired to consider their verdicts on 18 May 2001. It had been the most exhausting trial. The case just got more and more complex by the day. I certainly struggled to follow the plot, and I had no idea whether the jury kept up. How John got through it all without the support of a QC, I will never know.

Unfortunately, John's efforts had been in vain. Despite the staggeringly long trial, the jury didn't take long to find John and Christina guilty. He was now officially 'Britain's richest criminal'. Andrew walked free after jurors failed to agree a verdict on him.

John took off his watch and handed it to his solicitor before being led to the cells. After the theatre of the Brink's–Mat trial, there was no kiss for the jury this time. Christina was near to tears as she was remanded, presumably so she could go home to comfort their son. It was bad enough for my girls, but I did think of Christina's now teenage boy James, who had both his parents convicted on the same day. It was awful.

In mitigation, John told Judge Gerald Gordon: 'I acknowledge I have a strong, dominant personality, probably from my background. I have always relied on my wits for the benefit of those near and dear to me.'

But Gordon told him: 'The jury has heard from a number of elderly witnesses, many of whose retirements have been ruined as a result of the fraud.'

The next week John was sentenced. He knew he would be jailed, and said he didn't want me there. He told me he didn't want to put me through the pain, but I knew he didn't want the awkwardness of me being around Christina, too.

13

BUSTED

24 May 2001: What do you do on the morning your husband is being sent down, his reputation in tatters, the lead item on national news? I had no idea. As he wanted me nowhere near the Old Bailey, I tried to clear my mind by getting the groceries in at my local Asda supermarket!

It was bad enough knowing your husband was now a convicted fraudster, but it was doubly humiliating that his second life with Christina was now completely out in the open. I knew I would have to start again. On reflection, however, it was a bit drastic to do the weekly shop that same morning. I must have looked like a zombie as I pushed the trolley up the aisles, unable to think about anything but the scenes in Court 12.

I was in the queue to pay when my friend texted me: 'John has got eight years.'

I didn't know what to do with myself. I placed my fruit and veg on the supermarket belt and prepared to pay. The cashier didn't look up as she said: 'How has your day been?'

'Not too good,' I replied. 'My husband has just this minute been jailed.'

She looked at me open-mouthed and agog, but couldn't get a word out. I just did my best to place the veg in the carrier bags without bursting into tears.

I actually found it a relief to say it out loud. I no longer had to pretend things were okay or make out that this had been some big misunderstanding. Clearly, life at that point was a disaster; there was no point in denying that any more.

I am told John was close to tears as he was jailed for eight years. Christina was later given a two-year suspended sentence, which, despite all my ill-feeling, was a relief. James needed his mum around.

'I'll be out in four years,' John promised our daughters. He was right, but it would be the longest four years of his life.

His reputation made him a huge target on the wings of Britain's toughest jails. But his biggest problem of all was that detectives were convinced he was planning to escape. As a result the Ministry of Justice would make sure he would suffer.

John was shifted around jails faster than I could keep up. He was in solitary in Belmarsh, then Long Lartin, then back to Belmarsh. Now the authorities had got their man, they were going to make damn well sure he had a torrid time.

My husband, now in his mid 50s and jittery from life without cocaine, was a wreck. John had to wear a plastic orange suit with H (high security) emblazoned on his back. Every time I saw him inside he seemed to look another five years older. It was a ridiculous waste of everyone's time that he was being kept as a Category A prisoner.

I wrote to my local MP to question his jail conditions. He was useless, no help whatsoever, so I pursued the Home Secretary with a letter. Of course, they weren't interested. The Home Office wrote back to me just to say: 'Mr Palmer is a risk to the Crown.'

When I showed John the letters during a visit, he just threw them on the floor. 'Why should I care about this? I'm only being let out of the cell for one hour a day. Don't come to me with this unless you can help.'

Then, while he was inside, the petition for bankruptcy was launched by the timeshare victims. In a bid to fight the claims, he was duped into taking on crooked lawyer Giovanni Di Stefano. He had visited John in jail and told him everything he wanted to hear, but nothing that he needed to know. He boasted of representing train robber Ronnie Biggs, Slobodan Milošević and Saddam Hussein's legal team. I couldn't believe John trusted him. Everyone knew he had a dubious reputation. He was more likely to end up a cellmate than John's saviour. And as it turned out, Di Stefano was indeed jailed after being convicted of deception, fraud and money laundering.

He certainly did his bit to rip John off. Jason Coghlan, a former armed robber at Long Lartin jail, claimed Di Stefano had been using John's flat, and even borrowed his suits. Years later, Coghlan told *The Guardian* how he had recommended him to John while they shared a cell. He told the newspaper: 'Giovanni was staying at John's apartment in central London whilst handling his case at the high court and after one of the hearings Giovanni did a press conference, and when we all watched it on television that evening John started jumping up and down because Giovanni was wearing one of his suits – they're both short wee fellows!'

Meanwhile, in November 2001, John was named in the newspapers for helping Noye after the M25 stabbing of Stephen Cameron. It was claimed again that John had arranged Noye's flight by helicopter to a golf course at Caen, Normandy, and then by his private plane to Paris. John was enraged, but while he languished behind bars, he had no opportunity to set the record straight.

'The police have leaked this lie just to taunt me,' he said.

John continued to run his businesses from his jail cell but those four years inside changed so much. John needed a break from the cocaine, and I needed to work out whether I could build a life for myself. There was no way back for us.

A tipping point was the death of my mother in January 2003. She had been very unwell for some time, having had a nasty stroke the previous winter. She got some mobility back, but never her speech. My stepfather would bring her over and I would do her hair once a week. The last time I saw her, she had a bad stomach and I gave her a hot water bottle. She didn't seem quite right.

John, still behind bars, had made a big deal about paying £12,000 for a private jet to get me and the girls out to the *Brave Goose* over Christmas and New Year. I flew out with my youngest, Sammy, and her boyfriend to sail around Lanzarote. During the trip, a call came through to the captain from my stepfather.

'Marnie, it's your mum, she's fallen ill and has been rushed into intensive care in hospital,' he said. 'Please will you come home to see her? Your mother has been asking when are you coming? The doctors say she suffered an embolism. I've never seen so much blood.'

I packed my bags and prepared to arrange a flight back to Bristol when another call came through, this time from John in Long Lartin.

'What are you thinking of?' he yelled down the phone. 'You can't go home. You'll ruin Sammy's holiday.'

Reluctantly, I agreed to stay. By the time I ended up getting back to Britain, I had missed mum's death by three days.

I was stricken by guilt and grief. My relationship with her
had been as fraught as my relationship with John, but I should
have been there for her. It will be a regret to my own dying
day that I didn't fly back in time. My stepfather was devastated.
She was his everything. They were so committed to each other
– the relationship I once hoped John and I would have had.
I walked into the Chapel of Rest and wept: 'Sorry Mum –
I love you so much.'

A few weeks later I went to see John. Despite everything
he had put me through and all those people who had lost
their savings, I wanted to console him. I always believed I
was the one person who could help get him back on his
feet. He looked defeated and small as he sat hunched behind
a small metal table in the bleak prison meeting room. John
looked down at his handcuffed hands, and said: 'I feel like
I am cursed. There is a vendetta against me. Someone very
powerful is out to get me.' I believed him, and, for all the
hurt he had caused me, I still had to let him know I was on
his side. 'We know the truth John. You are taking the fall,
but you can bounce back. Forget about the police and the
papers. You can come back from this. You've done it before.'
He didn't respond.

'They're treating me like a beast, and I have no idea why,'
he said.

We later found out officers were bugging his calls.
I wondered whether something might have been said over
the phone to suggest he was an escape threat. I knew John
would never entertain the thought after the stress he had
endured when police caught him in Brazil in the 1980s, but
the governor clearly wasn't taking any risks.

John added: 'There are paedophiles and murderers in here,
yet it's me who gets treated like an animal.'

By 2003, the Crown was closing in on a confiscation order for £33 million of his assets. This was worse than the jail time for him. It was the biggest confiscation order in history, and he was absolutely raging about it. He also faced a potential multi-million-pound compensation case by the fraud victims.

'I don't have the money to pay that,' he told me. 'The figures are pie in the sky.'

I felt for those who had lost their money, all the pensioners that had given evidence in court. At first I consoled myself that at least they would get some of their hard-earned cash back.

But John told me: 'I bet you they barely get a penny from this. This will just be the government trying to rebalance the books after wasting tens of millions of pounds getting me convicted.'

This time John thought better of trying to fight the case himself. He hired a large legal team who filed dozens of files to the High Court protesting at the confiscation.

By May, it looked like he might be successful after an apparent blunder by Court of Appeal judges. They had thrown out the confiscation order because a paper served on him referred to the wrong section of an Act. Lord Woolf, sitting with four other judges at a special hearing, said the Court of Appeal had 'misunderstood and misapplied' the law and John's case had been 'wrongly decided'. As a result, Lord Woolf said John would be able to keep the cash because there was no legal way to make him hand it over.

By this stage the timeshare victims were as angry with the government as they were with John. A group of those who claimed they were owed cash came together to launch a bid to get him declared bankrupt as they pursued a separate £3.8 million compensation order issued by the

High Court. Sheffield-based firm Irwin Mitchell, representing 350 claimants, was driving the bid and John was defeated. He was formally declared bankrupt on 1 May 2005, with debts of £3.9 million.

Throughout most of John's first stint in jail in the early 2000s, I I was receiving regular payments to keep the house going. The sums weren't anything like the tens of thousands I might have expected in the '90s, but it was enough to keep the property ticking over as well as making sure my horses were fed. However, as I got by on the reduced amount, I was staggered to discover Saskia was set to receive a huge sum after a court battle surrounding maintenance for their son. John's solicitor accidentally sent all the documentation to my address instead of directly to John in prison. I didn't know the final figure, but the legal papers said she wanted £3 million. John said: 'The settlement will be nothing like that. I'll make sure that bitch doesn't get a penny.'

But he shouldn't have been so confident. He was eventually ordered by a judge to pay at least £70,000 a year to her in addition to an even bigger trust fund for their son, potentially worth millions. To ensure he paid her, the judge gave her shares in his timeshare business.

Most gruelling for everyone, however, was that he had also paid out £2.7 million to the Spanish government in taxes. The *Bristol Evening Post* interviewed a number of his victims. The duped investors raged about the payouts, saying every penny should have gone towards scam compensation.

One pensioner, 82-year-old John Davidson from York, said: 'Any money should go to people who have suffered, not the Spanish government. The whole thing is a disgrace … His victims have suffered far more than him.'

To be honest, it was hard to disagree with him.

Nick Wood, of accountancy firm Grant Thornton, was appointed trustee for the bankruptcy. Wood said: 'The creditors will get something back. But it's early days in the investigation so I shouldn't like to hazard a guess at how much they will receive.'

In fact, Wood and his firm would haunt the rest of John's life, and squeeze every penny out of him. At least the victims can rest assured at that, however painful it was for my husband.

At the time, John was at High Down Prison in Surrey. His name was now mud with anyone who had ever invested with him. John now needed every friend he could get, and our relationship improved. It may seem ridiculous after the violence, the betrayals and divorce petitions, but we still loved each other. We couldn't live with each other, but we certainly couldn't live without each other – well, at least not completely. There was never any chance of us sleeping in the same bed again, but we were at least speaking to each other with genuine warmth.

About six weeks before his release in the autumn of 2005, John phoned me from prison to tell me he was 'glad' he was being made bankrupt. 'Everything will be better, my love,' he said. 'The business can start again without the vultures circling. This is what I need. A clean break.'

I wasn't convinced. The gravy train had not only wobbled off the rails, it was now careering towards a great cliff edge.

A week or so after the call, a heavy package of documents landed with a thud on the doormat. It had 'Grant Thornton' stamped on the front. Before I had even opened it, I thought back to John's 'everything will be better' comment. The penny dropped: John had been buttering me up for this bombshell. I opened the envelope to read FREEZING ORDER in huge red type. It said my home, together with Christina's Fox Down Cottage, and even the *Brave Goose* and John's property portfolio in Spain were all up for confiscation. To say the least, John had been a trifle over-optimistic. Clearly we were going to lose lock, stock and barrel.

'The robbing bastards have got me this time,' he would say. 'I'll never have what we had again. I'm worn out.'

Around that time, I flew out for the last time to the *Brave Goose*. It was a great holiday, but I knew things were about to change. The boat was in the papers all the time. It would be a miracle if John was able to hold on to her, and he said he was planning to dismantle her. Indeed, she would be taken into the dry dock at Santa Cruz and pulled to pieces as the bankruptcy firms went to war on us. Eventually, Christina struck a deal with Grant Thornton to buy her back. She was back in the water by 2010.

At the time, however, we had to count the pennies for the first time since we were married. I kept the staffing receipt from the last time we stayed on there. For five days, the crew charged us £4,500. It was a big struggle to clear that bill. A few years ago we could have spent ten times that amount and it wouldn't have been a problem.

We had grown so attached to the crew back then. They were mainly Filipino and sending almost every penny they earned back to their impoverished families. I convinced John to help them get work elsewhere within the company when we could no longer afford to travel out to the boat.

Back home, his business interests were all but frozen. The shops in Bristol, Bath and Cardiff were closed down immediately. It was sad to see those businesses with the shutters down. Nobody could deny how hard John had worked to get himself set up. John had also lost his planes during his timeshare jail stint, and he was heartbroken when the Swedish firm called them in.

There were also a lot of people who needed paying on the property. My subsistence allowance from John's finances was gradually reduced to £600 a month and, eventually, nothing at all. I had to let everyone go. I had so many outgoings, but the horses were the biggest cost of all. I could no longer compete in elite events but the thought of losing these animals was heartbreaking.

People who had worked for us in the stables for decades were asked to leave. They were so kind and understanding. I was honest and said we had no more money, but they stayed until the horses were either sold off or put down.

I found it devastating walking out to the equestrian centre when they were all gone. The place was deserted. The magnitude of it all was starting to hit home.

Suddenly, after years of never even considering the price of things, I was acutely aware of how expensive our lavish lifestyle had become. I was almost ashamed of how wasteful we had been.

Of course, I had to sell anything and everything to keep going. I had auctioned off John's treasured Ferrari 275P. I remember our pal Martin picked it up and put it onto the loader – it was so sad to see it go. It went for auction at Sotheby's in London, and I remember them calling me up: 'Madam, it's fetched a price of £189,000. Does that sound acceptable?'

It was more than acceptable. That would be all I had to keep me and the girls going for years.

I knew life was going to change for good when John got out. A couple of weeks before he was freed, he stopped my jail visits because he said he was finding them too upsetting. He also said prison officers were reading his mail, so he asked me to send him notes inside magazines. I did this diligently, but I knew things weren't right.

John, who was moved between prisons several times during his stint, had been calling every few days, but the phone soon stopped ringing. At the same time, he had stopped my daughters visiting him in prison.

The lawyers were going to town on us to recover the money. Their staff flew out to Tenerife, demanding paperwork for every property belonging to him. All their travel and accommodation expenses were picked up by us as part of the confiscation order. It made John's blood boil. Within weeks, they were seizing everything we owned – tens of millions of pounds in property alone.

'They're the real vultures in all this,' John would say.

The most frustrating thing of all was that so many of the apartments were sold off at a pittance. It made me think of those that had lost all their money in timeshares. The victims were being sold short by the very same people in charge of clawing their cash back. Some of John's property in Tenerife was covered by a Spanish embargo and had been frozen – but other bits were auctioned off at paltry offers.

The government claimed John never paid tax; I know for a fact that's not true. John was forever moaning about tax, and I was the one filling out the cheques for him. Regular cheques were being sent out, on a monthly basis – usually around £14,000.

'Bloody luxury tax,' John would moan.

John was a beaten man, and when he was finally released he vowed to keep his nose clean. As he walked out of jail, he surrendered his passport but was told he would also face a bill from the Spanish tax authorities. Di Stefano released a statement on John's behalf saying: 'It is better he is out than in, because he can make a real effort to repay people genuinely owed money. Those that are not, we will vigorously contest.'

As part of John's 'clean break', I always suspected he was going to move in with Christina for good. John had already bought her a remote country home near Brentwood, Essex. Throwing money at his women, showering us with properties and gifts, had always helped him keep control of us. It would take a very strong woman to walk away from all that. However, splashing the cash was no longer an option for John. Instead, we would be lucky to keep the roof over our heads.

Two days after his long-awaited release, John came to the Coach House to tell me exactly where I stood. He pulled no punches. As soon as he sat down at the kitchen table, he started boasting that his son, from his relationship with Christina, had written to him every day. He was just full of it.

'James is so tall and a fantastic boxer. He's been signed up, the boy is going places,' he said, picking out a picture of his son from his wallet.

I pretended to admire the picture, but he was playing one of his cruel games. Though he didn't say these words, the message was loud and clear: 'You never gave me a son. You failed me. You're worthless.'

It was so hurtful. Our daughters were growing up so quickly. Both were such lively teenagers, filling the home with noise and laughter. During her teens, my eldest, Janie, had a number of lovely boyfriends and always made an effort to make sure I got to know them. Sammy also had a great boyfriend, Steve. Sammy was just 14 when they met but the pair of them have stayed together all this time. They now live very happily in London. It's so reassuring to know how fantastic they are for each other.

Despite our lovely girls, John was determined to prove life was better without me. When I finally asked whether he was ever going to move back in, he snapped, 'No, why would I want to live here, in this dump?'

I knew we were done, but had to be sure. I asked him straight, 'What about us?'

He yelled back: 'What about Christina? She's been looking after you. Don't you know that? Who do you think the money was coming from while I've been inside? Your fairy godmother?'

I had assumed the regular payments in my bank account had all been set up by John. To be told Christina was the one sending the cash was the final indignity.

'What happened, John?' I asked.

'Brink's-Mat happened. You know that, and you enjoyed the money. Nothing was ever going to be the same again for us.'

The house was still full of his stuff. Most of it I had kept for decades. Some of the clothes – including expensive suits – had been untouched since our house had been raided back in the mid 1980s.

'It's all got too many memories. Everything in here. Just ditch the lot,' he said.

John said he would eventually be going back to Tenerife, where Christina had been running the business while he had been inside.

'Perhaps it would be an idea if you were my mistress rather than her,' he said, half-joking.

Devastated and hurt, I travelled down to my stepfather's in Devon for Christmas. I cried like a lovesick teenager for almost the entirety of the two days I was there. I had wanted a divorce, but the callous way he spoke to me left me inconsolable. I felt so stupid.

My stepdad was a great help to me to me at this time. As it turned out, this would be a turning point for me. Yes, I was heartbroken, but my father helped me understand that it wasn't just John's feelings that had changed: this was my chance to escape all those years of betrayal and heartbreak.

A few weeks later, to cheer me up, my stepdad bought me a laptop computer. Amazing to think that my old dad was bringing me into the twenty-first century, but he knew it would keep my mind off things. And he was so right, as one of the first things I used it for was to join a dating site. I had stuck loyally by John for all these years, and now I was lonely.

This was a big breakthrough. I was at last thinking about the future, and not just obsessing about how to repair things with the girls and John.

My stepdad had moved out of the house he shared with my mum in Bristol, and found himself a bungalow back in Totnes. He was bereft after of the loss of my mother. I admired that he always loved her through thick and thin. However, in many ways, the loss of mum brought me together with him. We were grieving together and grew closer. It was the father–daughter relationship I had missed all my life. He forged a closer relationship during that time with Sammy as well. He would live for another decade and was a great support to me as my relationship with John and our financial situation became increasingly chaotic.

Thanks to my stepdad's support, I soon started to see John for what he was. It almost helped that he carried on acting a complete swine. John was becoming determined to make my life a misery because his own powers were diminishing. He was filled with resentment after being told by countless associates and police alike that he was a marked man.

John received a number of fresh death threats. Despite all his efforts to keep his business in line behind bars, he was now being cut completely out of the timeshare industry. Even Mohammed Derbah, previously his lieutenant, was ignoring his calls.

According to a July 2003 report in *The Observer*, police suspected Mo of laundering up to £500 million in Tenerife for gangs from Britain, Russia and South America. David Rose, the newspaper's correspondent, wrote of claims that Mo had even supplied weapons and money to the Amal and Hezbollah militias in Lebanon, and was involved in the theft of 1,300 French passports on behalf of al-Qaeda. However, there were never any follow up reports in the UK confirming whether Mo ever faced any charges. Equally there were so many claims of police corruption. I didn't know what to believe.

Within a few months of John's release, two remaining allies, Flo and Billy Robinson, were murdered. I didn't know them, but John had worked closely with them for years. According to reports, Billy and Flo had met senior manager Chris Collins and his wife for a meal at Teppenyaki, an upmarket Chinese/Japanese restaurant on the edge of Playas de las Americas. Having enjoyed their meal, they left for home about 10.30 p.m. An hour later they were dead.

Brutally murdered, their bodies were dumped at separate locations. Flo was found at 11.30 p.m. on 12 January 2006 in a pool of blood beside her silver Mercedes, on a single-track lane less than 300m from their villa at Oroteanda Alta in the San Miguel de Abona region. Billy's body was not discovered until the next morning, on the back seat of his gunmetal grey Porsche Cayenne on a bleak road behind an industrial estate, Las Chafiras, a few kilometres away.

Officially, police said Billy, 58, suffered multiple stab wounds, while Flo, 55, was bludgeoned to death. However, reports said the pair had both been tortured and their throats slit. Flo suffered horrific mutilation. I remember speaking to John about it on the phone from Bath after I read about it in the papers. All of the reports speculated about links with

John, but I half expected John to deny even knowing the couple. In fact, he was very sombre.

'I knew them well – they were very good friends,' he said. 'This is terrible.'

What worried John most was that there was no chance this was a robbery. A £100,000 gold watch remained on Billy's wrist, and Flo's diamond earrings were still in her ears. Whoever did this was sending a signal to potential timeshare bosses.

In recent years, the Robinsons had launched a business very much like John's. Global World Travel, incorporating a company called Timelinx, a sort of repackaged timeshare business, where customers bought into a whole-lifetime holiday package rather than the old much-maligned timeshare.

But John never held this against them; they had been loyal and loving friends. One theory is that the murderers got off the island that night or the next day. But they would have been drenched in blood, and would have needed a safe house in which to wash themselves and dispose of their clothes, and perhaps private transport to avoid airport CCTV and security checks. For John, this suggested the killers were from Africa or Russia – and they were sending out a message: 'Britons, get off our turf.'

Like so many crimes on the island, the murders were never solved. The police force that controlled the area had simply failed to keep up with the growth of the island's holiday industry. It was easier to let gangsters do their business behind the scenes and instead focus on big fish like John, the easiest of targets thanks to his previous brushes with the law.

By this time, John was travelling back to Tenerife only to get rid of his business interests there. Christina had even been working in one of the island's restaurants, El Faro, to keep the money coming in. Now it was her instead of John doing the commute backwards and forwards from Tenerife. As John's profile dwindled, Christina had become virtually the only point of contact for their former businesses.

John was no longer the biggest man in town – but it still suited police to paint him as a public enemy. Inspector Trinitario Sanchez, of the National Police, who specialised in investigating timeshare fraud, told the papers he was getting five or six reports a month of tourists being conned, usually British or Germans, and often elderly.

'Yet it's me who is marked the evil one,' John would say with a shrug. 'It's too much hassle for the Spanish to look at the Moroccans or the Russians. Far too dangerous. Why bother when they can stitch me up again?'

The Spanish police were desperate to lock him up again, and a source confirmed to us that they had been bugging phones while John had been inside in the UK. We worried they had found proof that John was still in charge of the business, despite serving time.

Our fears were proved right in July 2007. John, then 57, was arrested by Madrid detectives as he landed on a jet from London at Reina Sofia airport, Tenerife. He was grabbed by police as he waited for his luggage, then taken to a police station before being quickly transferred to Madrid to face the country's most high-profile investigating magistrate, Judge Baltasar Garzón.

Police told him they believed his operations went much further than British authorities had thought, and admitted their evidence was based on those prison phone chats between John and 'known criminals' on Tenerife.

Garzón, we learned, was obsessed with John, and prepared to go to any lengths to get a conviction. In hindsight, my husband should have pulled the case apart on the basis of the wiretapped evidence. In 2012, the magistrate was found guilty of abuse of power in a separate case for ordering the illegal wiretapping between lawyers and suspects in a corruption investigation that implicated members of the ruling Popular Party. The penalty was suspension from the bench for eleven years, effectively ending the career of a judge who won global renown by trying to extradite Chile's former dictator Augusto Pinochet from London in 1998. The court said: 'Garzón's methods are typical of totalitarian countries, without any respect of the right of defence.'

However, at the time of his arrest, in 2007, John and his legal team had no idea what Spanish authorities were allowed to do. The charges he faced in Spain were potentially far more serious than those he faced in the UK. Officers working for Garzón said John was 'wanted by the court for being the (suspected) leader of an international criminal group based on the island'.

Officers believed he was leading a violent organised crime group involved in fraud, money laundering, drug trafficking, bribing public officials, possessing firearms and falsifying passports and credit cards. The specialist plain clothes Spanish police had been tailing him for weeks, but were only able to make their arrest once he had landed. In a statement, police said:

> John Palmer is considered to be the head of a criminal organisation which operated from Tenerife, dedicated to multiple criminal activities.
>
> You can calculate in hundreds of millions of euros the criminal benefits obtained by this gang in the last few years. He has investments in Tenerife and the Costa del Sol worth more than £244 million … From prison he managed and controlled the entire criminal network.

John and I were talking regularly at this time. He was ringing me at home every couple of days, either for my opinion or just to vent. He needed the advice of people he could trust – and there were not many of those allies left by this stage. 'It's all such a stitch up,' he said in a phone call from custody. 'The worst of this is that by arresting me it allows all the real villains to get away with it all. They are pursuing me simply because it makes them look good. They don't care about the truth.'

Police estimated his empire in the Canary Islands was worth about €360 million (£245 million at the time). To us, that was a laughable figure. Since the creditors had arrived, John barely had a bean left. Only £3.9 million of debts were declared when he was formally made bankrupt in 2005 – and the lawyers hadn't left a penny of it.

Yet John was the headline arrest for this new investigation into the criminal underworld on the island. The new Mr Bigs on the island were now too dangerous, so they went for John, who was relatively easy pickings after his British jail stint.

After his arrest, John was taken to a local police station and held overnight before being flown to Madrid to appear at the National Court. The indictment said John's business was 'a machine for carrying out timeshare fraud between 1993 and 2002', and it was run 'under his orders' after he was jailed. It said John's gang sold tourists timeshare in apartments never built. Others handed over money to be invested, but never saw it again. A lot of it was the same old evidence from British detectives, but the Spanish reckoned they had more proof. One tapped call suggested one of his lieutenants had boasted he made £12 million after John put him in charge of the organisation.

Despite hearing all this evidence, John wasn't charged. Instead, he was kept festering in jail for more than three years while the Spaniards prepared their case. I'd heard of *mañana*, but this was ridiculous. He had a dreadful time, and said it was worse than British jails – dirtier, and swelteringly hot. Again, prison guards were put on alert for an escape bid. Because of his connections, he would be kept isolated in prisons and moved around a lot. He was mostly in a cramped cell near Madrid.

The prosecution against him was so strange. There was no big trial like in the UK; instead, there seemed to be loads of smaller court dates, and they just kept him in jail between each. One judge told him he would be incarcerated for eight years, while another said he would be in for a year. The officials were also moving him around jails across Spain almost every month. The crumb of comfort keeping him going all that time was that Garzón, the magistrate who had been pursuing him so relentlessly, was now facing jail himself. It gave John hope that the case against him would some day collapse.

He refused to see me or my daughters for the entirety of this third jail stint. Sammy begged him to change his mind but Christina and her son were using up a lot of the visiting time. The treatment was incredibly hurtful, but again, I sent him letters hidden in magazines so the screws would not take them away.

Still the bankruptcy firms were threatening to ruin us. The letters kept piling up while John was inside, but I did everything I could to keep hold of the Coach House. If I lost that I would have nothing when our divorce was finally agreed.

John was eventually released on bail in the winter of 2011. Spanish police were still waiting to decide whether he would be tried. In fact, it would be May 2015 before they made up their minds. John would be charged again with Christina and Andrew. Another nephew, Darren Morris, was also named on the sheet. Investigative magistrate Pablo Ruz Gutierrez had taken over the probe, and claimed a 9mm Zastava pistol, seized in a raid in Tenerife, belonged to John.

After his release, John surprised me by flying back to the Coach House on the first plane he could book. I had expected him to go to Christina and James. But there was never any hope that this surprise visit was to see me and the girls. There was another, more pressing reason for his trip back to Bath. John was searching for something near the gates at the bottom of the drive. I remember him stood there in heavy snow as I watched him on the CCTV. He was staring at a camera, as though he didn't want me to see. Then he got in his car and drove past the camera, before his wheels got chewed up in the snow. He phoned the house and asked Janie's boyfriend Red to come and help with a rope. This was the second time he had been stuck in that remote corner of our grounds.

Still to this day, I am not sure what this was about. John wouldn't tell any of us what he was up to. At the time, I thought it may have been a personal drugs stash, but John would probably have been more open about that. And, at the time, he claimed he was off the coke. It's more likely that he was looking for one of the spots where he had hidden cash. These were desperate times. He needed every penny.

Whatever was there, John really didn't want us to know. Refusing to say what he was looking for, he came back into the kitchen and made some phone calls. He wolfed down a sandwich and looked like he was preparing to leave.

But then he sat down again at the table and stared up at me. He looked so downbeat. For the first time since his mum had died, he looked ready to cry.

'I've lost everything,' he said. 'I'm driving around in a banger. The police want to take the clothes from my back.'

He then looked around the room to see what possessions of his I had kept. 'I've got rid of it all, like you told me to,' I told him.

All those clothes, jewellery and furniture had been auctioned off for anything I could get. 'I had to pay the bills here, John. You're not the only one suffering.'

John replied: 'I'm a bankrupt. I'm nothing.'

The tears were in his eyes. It was the most vulnerable I have ever seen him. 'You'll get back on your feet, John,' I told him. 'You always do.'

John said he needed to go back to Tenerife. There were huge problems to sort out. Janie was terrified by this prospect.

'Dad, please don't go,' she said. 'Please don't go.'

John had desperation in his eyes, as though he knew something was about to go terribly wrong. 'I've no choice. I have to sort out everything in Tenerife. If I don't go, I'll lose it all.'

Despite all the betrayals and bloodshed, I felt awful for John. It was terrible to see him so defeated. There was something seriously troubling him. Fighting back my own tears, I went upstairs and retrieved the one thing I thought I would never part with: a huge diamond ring John had given me after my original engagement ring had been stolen. I had only ever worn it when we had gone to the fanciest restaurants for meals. It was my prize possession. When John gave it to me I vividly remember him saying: 'You enjoy it, but look after it – this is your protection on a rainy day.'

'Well, this is that rainy day,' I said to John as I handed it back to him twenty years later. He was grateful and said he would give me the money back.

'Okay, John, when you're back on your feet,' I said. Deep down, I knew I wouldn't ever see a penny from that diamond.

Then, in our most honest exchange in years, John admitted everything. All the cheating and the affairs. It was just confirmation of what I already knew. Even though I was resigned to divorce and glad to be moving on, I needed to hear from him that our marriage was completely over.

I asked him: 'What is going to become of us? What about me?'

He just replied: 'I'm never coming back to you. We're done.'

I also confronted him about the reports of violence – all those horrible rumours of people being beaten up because they owed John money for the timeshare business. We had never spoken about this before, but he would come home with marks on his hands. I knew he had hit people and could be a violent man.

'You never wanted to know,' he said. 'You enjoyed the money and the lifestyle, and that's okay.'

Still to this day I cannot bring myself to believe John was that nasty, horrible person portrayed by police and the press. But do I know hand on heart? No, I will never know the whole truth. He laughed off the allegations for years. He became so used to defending himself that sometimes he would forget what the truth was.

14

DOOMED

After three and a half years in Spanish jails, John cut a forlorn figure for months after his release. He was increasingly bitter and twisted over the creditors, and he had lost so much weight in his face. He was gaunt, grey and in pain, plagued by stomach and chest complaints. All those years of stress and excess had taken their toll. My now estranged husband looked like an old man.

John finally moved back to the UK full time, apparently cutting all ties with Tenerife. He and I only had intermittent contact as he became more and more reclusive, living with James and Christina at their cottage on sprawling grounds in South Weald, near Brentwood.

The prospect of another trial was too much. His health was failing, too. I'm told John would often prowl around his Essex home, deep in thought. Previously, he was so noisy, the life and soul of any gathering. Now he was like wounded prey, running out of space to hide. After previous setbacks, he was always planning the next comeback.

He knew he had to pick himself up one last time, even though the creditors had him on his knees. He was not quite defeated. Christina still had a restaurant in Tenerife, but John vowed to put any business interests there behind him. Instead he went back to what he knew best: selling jewellery and gold.

He amazed us all by his return to the trade after thirty years. The game had changed so much while he had been away, but it was still the industry he knew best.

He managed to pull together enough cash for a jewellers in Kensington, West London. It was a flash place around the corner from Harrods. I thought it would be a big success, but the antiques world had changed even more than John had expected. With the boom in online trading, the overheads involved in a West End jewellers were a ridiculous waste.

He walked away from the shop and instead worked with Christina on a pawnbrokers and jewellers that operated in Essex, but also online.

Essex Pawn Stars, registered in Christina's name, was selling watches for as much as £25,000, and offering loans against luxury valuables from £1,000 to £100,000. Essex Pawn Stars used Twitter and Instagram – social media unknown to me – to advertise some lovely Cartier and Rolex watches, and were reportedly attracting a host of reality television star customers.

Online trading was very new to John, but, with Christina and James's help, I believed he could thrive again. Dealing bullion was always his passion. Gold had rocketed in value since the 1980s. Umicore Feingold pure gold bars were being sold at £2,620 for 100g. The mind boggles to think what that Brink's-Mat gold would be worth these days.

By that point, he had a new number two working for him; Rikky had been in jail with John. Rikky and I actually got on very well. When John was in one of his moods, Rikky would often fill me in on what was going on. He insisted John was now off the cocaine, which was a relief.

Rikky would drive John everywhere, and became his right-hand man. They worked closely together on jewellery deals and also traded a few cars online. I was amazed by this. It was just like John and Garth all those years ago.

John's other great hope of redemption was his son – James really was the apple of his eye. He helped get James a flat in Birmingham and was so proud as he studied for his accountancy degree. John was desperate to ensure his life would be free from all the strife and trouble with police that we had endured.

Our marriage was now over in all but writing, but I would see John when he came down to visit the girls, or check on the Coach House. Now he always had a laptop with him so he could buy and sell his gear. He would sit in the kitchen, busily tapping away. It reminded me of decades earlier when he was sketching those plans for timeshares on notepads.

Despite being wracked with worry and ill health, John had always taken pleasure from work. We were on difficult terms but he helped me and the girls with a small agriculture venture using the land at Battlefields. We bagged up a load of wild garlic and produce from the gardens to sell at Billingsgate Market, and to the restaurants.

With so many people after his money, he was doing as much as he could to raise cash in hand. A lot of businesses and property were also switched to Christina's name. She has a far better business brain than me; she was running things as much as John during those later years.

But the money he was making now was a pittance compared to the old days. There was no chance all these small ventures were going to keep the wolf from the door. In fact, they appeared to be riddled with debts. Six UK limited companies owed creditors a total of £914,219, with a value of -£230,269, according to Companies House records reported in the *Daily Express*.

I felt far from sorry for John. I had been forced to put the divorce on hold because John was refusing to sign the financial agreement. He said he was happy as things were and he would repeatedly play mind games with me. My solicitor warned me it would be a long and tortuous campaign of court hearings to get what I needed.

John's depression made him increasingly bitter and twisted, and he was gleefully causing a rift between me and my daughters over the sale of our property. It was all part of his campaign to turn the girls in his favour rather than mine.

As children, the girls would have sided with me, whatever the situation. I was the one that was there whenever they needed a parent. John was away so often, only coming home in short bursts, and behaving so unpredictably when he was there. As adults, however, they saw him differently. I was no longer the one they trusted, and now John was losing his money and was portraying himself as victim. In his depiction, I was the greedy one for trying to hold on to our home.

He tried to convince my daughters to fight me for a stake in our property. Of course, I wanted to help them, but I still needed a roof over my head.

John did once confide in me that his worst fear was that Janie would end up an addict like he was. That was his worst worry of all, he said. Yet despite caring for her so much, John was so selfish in his attempts to drive her away from me. It certainly didn't help our daughter. She was so fragile, she needed her mother around. We had supported each other for years.

Janie's love life was even more eventful than my own before our rift. She met an Italian in Lanzarote who I quite liked, but when that fizzled out she quickly met a Londoner and lived with him for a while. When they broke up after several months, she wanted to stay with me. Eventually, John suggested she should move into Chapel Cottage adjoining the Coach House.

John knew this would hamper my plans for the place. I had planned to extend our home into it, but John had turned it into his 'surveillance' office. He had a full-time member of staff who would come and go from the property, reviewing CCTV footage. Before we had even split up, I was refused access to the locked rooms where the footage was kept. The estate manager was reporting my movements, as well as any developments on the estate, back to my paranoid husband, even when he was behind bars. John had become so used to being under the twenty-four-hour watch of police that he obviously decided others deserved a taste of this medicine. It was very unnerving.

Now Janie was back, too. For John, this was a second useful spy on my activities. He loved the control. John agreed to convert the place into a nice living space again and I went away on holiday.

When I returned a fortnight later, Janie had moved in – with Red, a new man I had never even met before. Janie had introduced me to other boys but she clearly wanted to keep me at a distance from Red. For some reason, she was very keen to avoid giving me a chance to rule over him.

The new boyfriend had apparently moved into the cottage within days, and John took an almost instant dislike to him. John would grumble about him being useless, and he eventually ordered Red to paint the outside of the cottage in a bid to make him earn his keep. Amazingly, he did paint it. John was more accepting after that.

Red and Janie had regular fights. It was a very chaotic time, and things came to a head when I told them both that I couldn't put up with the constant rows, and it might be best if they left.

In the background, however, John was stirring it all up. He was constantly telling the girls that my home was their inheritance. With that in mind, there was no way Janie would agree to leave.

He would use this tension with my daughter to his advantage. He drove a wedge between us that we would never recover from. Over the years, he had beaten me, cheated on me and had even held a gun to my head – but turning my own children against me was the worst betrayal of all.

He set about dismantling everything I tried to do. John would do whatever he could to exert his power, even disrupting work that went on in the house. In 2012, the flat roof in the bathroom fell in. It was a nightmare, as we couldn't even afford to have it repaired. We had to leave it for weeks while John kept delaying about whether he would help us. Eventually he said he would pay, so I booked in a contractor. Then John changed his mind halfway through the job. All of a sudden, I had no way to pay the poor builder. John messed about for weeks, before eventually paying up.

There were so many outgoings, and the neighbours were constantly harassing us about getting rotting fences repaired around our grounds. John would stir it all up.

'Don't you worry, I'll pay for it all,' he would tell them. Then, looking at me, he would add with a smirk: 'Marnie, you must look after these people.'

Then, when we got back to the Coach House, it was a different story again. 'I'm not paying a bloody penny … you pay for it yourself.'

It was all just a laugh and a joke for John, but he knew he was grinding me down. By that stage, I really think he hated me. He would constantly lie to me.

In August 2012, he arrived out of the blue with a trailer carrying a horse.

'Marnie, can you take care of him for a few weeks? He belongs to a racehorse trainer I know who's fallen on hard times.'

He must have thought I was born yesterday. I knew full well that Christina had recently fallen off a horse. I was sure he had lumbered me with this animal because she no longer wanted to look after it.

I knew he was lying, but my heart is like butter when it comes to horses – it melted as soon as I saw him. John sent me a bit of money to look after him, but the animal's behaviour was dangerously erratic. He injured himself running through a fence, and we eventually had to have him put down.

Money was tighter than it had ever been. I sold everything I could to keep the house going. Almost every antique and painting in the property had already gone. John agreed to buy any remaining jewellery, but at a fraction of its real value.

Selling the estate was inevitable, but I was sure John, in his current state, would make it difficult. We had always agreed the house would be mine, and it was my name on the deeds. For all John's tough talk, he knew I was in the right on this.

Given this Mexican standoff, I was amazed when he eventually told Janie he would buy her a house so she could move out of the cottage adjoining our home. I thought this offered a glimmer of hope that I could put the house on the market.

John laughed when I told him I was selling up, telling me: 'Yeah, you should move somewhere easier. I saw a programme the other day about old ladies not being able to look after their homes.'

He was being so spiteful, but I was simply glad he wasn't standing in my way. I initially advertised the property with Savills estate agent for just under £2 million, and there was plenty of interest until the agent called me to say John had been on the phone.

'Mrs Palmer, unfortunately your estranged husband claims there is a dispute over ownership so we cannot take the sale any further,' the agent said.

I was absolutely furious. By now he had cut off any financial support to help look after the Coach House's grounds, yet he still wanted to disrupt the sale.

The row then deepened as Janie told John she would rather stay at Chapel Cottage because Battlefields was her childhood home. I knew John had been winding her up to say this. He knew it was another chance to undermine me. Now she was determined to stay put, whatever I offered her. Our relationship hasn't recovered since, which is exactly what John wanted.

With the house on and off the market, and the dispute with Janie rumbling on, it would take three years to find a buyer. We dropped the price repeatedly out of desperation. John was constantly in my ear, telling me that I was selling it too cheap, but there was no way we could get more when it was falling into disrepair.

In 2013, my beloved stepfather died, and my row with Janie and John deepened even further. My stepdad was one of my few remaining allies. I was distraught to lose him. We buried him at Buckfastleigh, South Devon. My daughters came, and after the funeral, John confronted me to see what he had left for the girls. When I told him nothing, he went spare. He said I should pay my two daughters £45,000 each, there and then. Of course, that was impossible for me. Afterwards he demanded that I give the girls a huge stake of the Coach House sale instead.

The girls sided with him because he wound them up so much about it. John eventually demanded an £800,000 stake of the Coach for them, which was impossible. I would have loved to give the girls all the money they wanted, but I knew I had to protect myself. If I had provided what they were demanding, I would not have been able to buy a home for myself. The value of the property was already plunging as the place fell further into disrepair.

With the split with John, and our third attempt at divorce dragging along at a snail's pace, tensions reached boiling point. I was at the end of my tether with John and my daughters. I ended up making a very dramatic decision – evicting Janie and Red. My solicitor advised that serving notice on them would be the only way to achieve a quick sale. So, in the spring of 2013, I obtained a court order to get possession of Chapel Cottage. They were given twenty-eight days to leave, but appealed.

The case would rumble on for another two years. It was so awful dragging this all out. There were countless legal threats, and times where I thought I was going to lose everything.

I'm pretty sure John was paying Janie's solicitor fees and advising her on what to say. There were so many trips back and forwards to court. The fees were ridiculous, and nobody was gaining anything.

Janie's case to fight the eviction was that my daughters should be guaranteed £400,000 each from the sale of the property. It was a ridiculous suggestion. The property we were living in was falling apart before our eyes. We kept lowering the price. In the end we were lucky to get just over a £1 million for it.

Of course, you want to look after your children – that goes without saying. Against legal advice, just to put it behind us, I approached one of their lawyers and said I would give the girls £200,000. It was a generous offer, but they were greedy. They wrote back to my lawyer: 'As far as your client's offer is concerned, our clients are extremely upset, as they have been throughout the course of this matter, that your client has yet again failed to keep up to what has previously been agreed and continues with possession proceedings.'

I was gobsmacked when they turned my offer down. It was a huge mistake on their part to refuse me, as the court ruled again in my favour: I didn't owe them a penny. It was a victory with no winners. I still regret that it all became so poisonous.

In the end, just to get the Coach House sold, I paid Janie and Red £30,000 as a settlement for the 'work' that had been done there. It was a grossly inflated figure, but I couldn't see another option. Fortunately, they moved out as soon as the cheque cleared.

*

This was just a couple of months after the last time John ever came to the house, on 22 December 2014. John was in a terrible state, sweating buckets and nipping to the toilet every five minutes. Our relationship was at an all-time low but, out of habit if nothing else, I made dinner for us, Janie and Sammy.

As we sat down to eat our turkey, John looked dreadful. So pale and grey. He had been in and out of the bathroom retching. Eventually he admitted that he had gallbladder problems and gastroenteritis.

'I was in hospital a few weeks ago in intensive care,' he told us. 'I should have told you but I didn't want to worry you all.'

Too right he should have said. I knew the real reason he had kept quiet was that Christina would have been there at his bedside and he didn't want the awkwardness. But that was no excuse for failing to tell our daughters. He was so selfish.

After all those years of red wine and whisky, John was now drinking white wine, his idea of the healthy option. We teased him about that, and the meal was relatively cordial until John mentioned payouts for the girls again. Then I snapped. I couldn't take it any more, so I dashed towards the kitchen. I didn't want to give John the benefit of seeing me cry.

John then bellowed through the door that the whole house was our daughters' inheritance. He added that he didn't believe my stepfather had left them no money and that he suspected I had forged his will. Of course I hadn't, but, to twist the knife, he said: 'Even your parents turned their back on you. Do you not think your daughters will do the same when they realise what you're like?'

He even raged at me about our dog, Alli, who had recently been put down. I loved that dog, but he had been very ill. Yet Janie had told John I had him put to sleep simply because I couldn't be bothered to look after the animal. It had become so bitter between us.

'You WILL do as I say,' John yelled. 'Give our daughters their money out of the house.'

His eyes were bulging. I had seen him like this many times before. I could predict the precise moment he would completely lose the plot. He then pulled two £10 notes out of his pocket and threw them in my direction through the kitchen doors. 'That's all you're getting out of me.'

By now, both of us had signed the divorce papers. It was completely over, but there was no way to cut our ties completely while bankruptcy proceedings were ongoing. All his assets were frozen and there was no way to carve up what was mine. Still, to this day, this hasn't been completely resolved.

A few weeks later, a mutual friend had come to me with a message from John: he was offering me £1 million if I would agree to hand over the property to him. By that stage, there was no trust between us, and he had woven so many lies that I couldn't believe he was willing to make things easy. Just weeks before, he hadn't a penny to his name.

Then I got a text message to ring John on the landline from Chapel Cottage. We couldn't speak at the Coach House because he thought we were being bugged by police. John was very paranoid. We may have been under surveillance, but in this case I think he had mistaken clicking on the phone for me putting his conversations on loudspeaker when he was calling me a 'bitch'.

I did as I was told, however, and phoned him from the cottage. As soon as he picked up, John was ranting and raving about the house sale. He kept asking about the money for the girls and what I was going to do make things right. Under his terms, I would have been lucky to walk away from the whole marriage with £400,000. Enough to get a roof over my head but it was a pretty paltry offer from a man once reportedly worth £300 million.

'I can't afford that, John! The house is all that I have,' I yelled down the phone. 'I will be lucky if the house sells for a million. How on Earth will I make ends meet if I have to give it all away?'

Then I slammed down the receiver. It would be the last time I ever spoke to him.

15

DIAMOND WHEEZERS

New 'Crime of the Century', same old suspects. The Hatton Garden heist and Brink's-Mat bullions were separated by thirty-two years, but had so much in common. It was another ready-made script for Hollywood, and yet again the newspapers suggested there were suspicions my husband was in some way connected.

Dad's Army, The Diamond Wheezers … call them what you like, but give these pensioners their dues: the Easter 2015 bust in London's jewellery quarter had more front than Weston-super-Mare.

I read the reports with open-mouthed fascination; it was a throwback in time to those audacious raids of the 1980s. This was analogue rather than digital, a crime from a bygone era. I remember thinking John was bound to at least know of those involved.

Most astonishing of all was the involvement of 76-year-old Brian Reader, the same fella that served a nine-year stretch for delivering that Brink's-Mat bullion to Scadlynn in 1984 as an accomplice of John's. I was sorry to read that Reader had prostate cancer. Two years before, he had fallen out of a tree that he was cutting back on his property and fractured his neck. He had also recently lost his beloved wife. You might have thought he could barely leave the house, let alone rob an underground vault.

Yet Reader's impressive array of contacts would be key in once again turning loot into cold hard cash. Over pints of lager and glasses of vodka and tonic, the men would gather at the Castle Pub on Pentonville Road each Friday to iron out the details. With a huge amount of criminal experience under their belts, the gang knew they needed to plan for every eventuality, and also be prepared for the unexpected. As the date of the raid approached, mobile phone data showed how the gang were in almost constant contact, discussing how the job would unfold.

On Thursday, 2 April, following months of painstaking research and planning, the gang assembled, ready to strike at the heart of London's world-famous jewellery district. Reader, who didn't have a mobile phone or a car, used someone else's Travelcard to get from his home in Dartford to Clerkenwell, meeting up with the others in St John Street, around a five-minute walk from Hatton Garden.

At 6 p.m. on the Thursday evening, the security guards locked the vault in the Hatton Garden Safe Deposit Company and set the alarms. With the long bank holiday weekend stretching out before them, they expected the building to remain empty until first thing on Tuesday morning. At around 8.20 p.m., a white transit van, driven by John 'Kenny' Collins, arrived in Hatton Garden and parked up in Leather Lane around the corner from their target. The gang were dressed in high-visibility clothing and overalls, appearing to any unsuspecting passers-by to be workmen carrying out vital maintenance over the quiet holiday weekend.

Despite successfully breaching the concrete wall, the gang were only halfway home, and were now faced with the back of the metal cabinet that sat directly behind the wall and housed the individual safe deposit boxes. They had come prepared, bringing with them a hydraulic ram, but after several hours of intense work and little progress, the gang shattered the base of their equipment.

At this stage, two of the team, Reader and Carl Wood, decided that they'd had enough: the risks were too great. But the others returned with a new drill the next day and bored a hole 20in deep, 10in high and 18in through to the vault. Five of the gang ransacked seventy-three safe deposit boxes, grabbing almost £25 million in jewels, gold and cash. With the help of William 'Bill' Lincoln', they got the goods to Enfield, where they were split up. Most of the loot vanished and, it seemed initially, that they had got clean away.

With the raid making headlines around the world, Scotland Yard's Flying Squad came under intense pressure to find those responsible. John knew he would be a suspect simply because of his reputation. He was back in the country at the time and back in the jewellery business. I'm told he was surprised officers didn't come calling.

In the end, it was as easy as pie for police. Like Brink's-Mat, the gang had made huge blunders in attempting to cover their tracks. One member had given detectives the lead they needed by using his own distinctive white Mercedes car to carry out a reconnaissance sweep, while another member had used his real name at the DIY store where the gang purchased their drill on the weekend of the raid.

Police now knew exactly who was responsible, but they bided their time before swooping. Officers saw an opportunity to harvest a huge amount of intelligence about the underworld. They placed listening devices in cars and even in pubs.

Eventually they made their arrests and, following a trial at Woolwich Crown Court, Carl Wood and Lincoln were found guilty of conspiracy to commit burglary and conspiracy to conceal, convert or transfer criminal property, while Hugh Doyle was convicted of concealing, converting or transferring criminal property. Four men – Reader, Terry Perkins, John Collins and Daniel Jones – had already pleaded guilty to their part.

While most of them were jailed for up to seven years, one accomplice remained at large: 'Basil', on whose head there was a £20,000 reward. The mystery technical brains behind the raid, he had used keys and his specialist burglar alarm skills to pave the way for the mob to enter the Hatton Garden vault. However, with thousands of hours of bugged intelligence now in the hands of police, it seemed his co-conspirators had never identified him. He did not associate with the rest of the gang afterwards, and never communicated with them by phone, leaving no trail. Michael Seed, 57, the son of a Cambridge biophysicist, was arrested at a council flat in March 2018. He was awaiting trial as this book went to print.

One hilarious theory in the papers at the time was that Basil could be John. Inevitably, given his association with Reader, the newspapers would be bursting with speculation. But the Basil rumour was the most laughable theory imaginable. 'The press obviously haven't seen his belly very recently,' I thought. The thought of John squeezing his portly frame through that tiny hole they used to get into the vault was ridiculous. Police were watching his every move at the time. He would have shone up like a beacon to officers if he was directly involved.

However, there was a more plausible line of enquiry linking John with that heist: there were rumours knocking around

Hatton Garden that he had a box there that the raiders might have been looking for. I think this might well be right. Usually his most precious items were kept under lock and key at home, but, with a court case hanging over his head, I know John had a couple of safety boxes.

What struck me was a conversation I had with John when he was mouthing off about Irwin Mitchell, a firm of solicitors, eighteen months earlier. John was so furious about the way his empire had been dismantled and then sold off, way below asking price.

'They're robbing bastards, but I'll get them,' he said. 'I've got everything they've said on tape and receipts of all their spending. I'm going to prove how corrupt they are. They'll get what's coming to them.

'I'm just waiting for the right time. I've got them bang to rights. It's all under lock and key in a safety box.'

Now, I wonder whether he might have been spotted stashing his bag in Hatton Garden; he was such a known face in that area. He would have struggled to move a muscle without the knowledge being passed immediately into the powerful underworld network that still exists in that area of London.

You didn't have to be one of the golden oldies to know about John. And gossip always spread like wildfire, particularly amongst all those old cons with nothing more to do than meet up with their old mates 'giving it the big 'un' in the boozers of North London.

Did the whole Hatton Garden raid come about because Reader and his crew had heard about a potential Palmer stash in there? Seems far-fetched, but it's not impossible, especially if they were under the misapprehension that there was Brink's-Mat gold in one of the boxes. Reader would be more alert than most to the prospect that John might still have some of that loot. If so, they must have been pretty gutted to find John's box containing just a load of boring cassettes and documents about the taxman.

★

Then, of course, eleven weeks after the raid: John's death. Coincidence? We may never know.

CCTV footage at 5:18 p.m. showed John heading towards his purpose-built office, a short distance from the house. The area was virtually the only part of the property not covered by cameras.

Unbeknown to him, a hole had been cut in the fence near to the building, which enabled the shooter to watch him.

John started a little bonfire and was idly throwing paperwork into the blaze when he was confronted. The mystery gunman, brandishing an 8mm pistol, jumped over the fence, leaving scuff marks. He then shot John six times in the front and back. John staggered back towards the house, but got no more than 15m before he collapsed and died.

Being told this about the man you knew better than any other is almost surreal. Plunged into sudden grief, you can only immediately grasp for an explanation. However, the unanswered questions in this case were endless for me, and all his loved ones. Certainly, we were scratching our heads over Essex Police's ineptitude in failing to realise for a week that he had been murdered. But that paled into insignificance with the mind-boggling, sleep-depriving confusion of trying to work out which of John's countless enemies had killed him.

For police, there were two most likely scenarios: either that John was killed over some sort of Hatton Garden connection or, alternatively, that someone feared he was leaking information ahead of his fraud and racketeering trial in Spain. According to a report on the Mirror website, Christina, and nephews Andrew Palmer and Darren Morris were also facing fresh timeshare fraud charges alongside John.

As murder squad officers desperately attempted to make up lost ground in their investigation, DCI Stephen Jennings set public speculation into overdrive by telling the press:

> There are two very significant main lines of inquiry at the moment, the first being that John was due to stand trial in mainland Spain relating to real estate fraud that followed an eight year investigation. The second is a combination of factors throughout 2015 which included a number of significant crimes in the UK, significant law enforcement intervention into organised crime in the UK, and significant arrests of people in organised crime groups.

Behind the scenes, however, officers seemed as uncertain as us. Clearly, like me, they were convinced Basil was not John. However, I did get the impression they believed some sort of Hatton Garden link was more likely than a Spanish-ordered attack. The first Hatton Garden heist arrests began from 19 May, just over a month before John was gunned down. Around that time there were repeated reports that John might have turned supergrass. Anyone that knew him would never believe such a slur, but for those still fencing the loot, perhaps leaving him alive wasn't a risk worth taking.

Coincidences do happen, but everything did seem rather close for comfort, especially as John had been back in the country and back in the jewellery trade. I became even more suspicious when the *Mail on Sunday* published claims that John may well have been shot dead by a hitman working for one of London's most feared crime families over the 'supergrass' rumour.

Essex Police initially echoed my suspicions, but, after a few months of fruitless questioning, officers told me the trail had gone cold. When Reader and his gang were jailed in March 2016, detectives amended their position on John, admitting there could be thousands of potential killers. It felt like the investigation was going backwards.

By December 2016, eighteen months after the murder, detectives confirmed they were still no closer to solving the case. DCI Jennings spoke again at an inquest into John's death. He said that since launching the inquiry, they had pursued 700 lines of enquiry and taken 200 witness statements.

DCI Jennings said: 'We are not even close in terms of finishing this inquiry ... Because of Mr Palmer's lifestyle and his previous involvement with criminality, this has made it extremely extensive.'

In total, the detective said officers had uncovered '16,000 potential motives' for killing John. Now, clearly, his death seemed just as likely to be linked to the timeshare fraud and possibly even Brink's-Mat. Several people 'would have a legitimate motive of wanting to cause him harm', DCI Jennings added. In terms of underworld enemies, John could have given Al Capone a run for his money. Out of desperation, police offered a £50,000 reward to catch the killer.

I couldn't cope with the thought of attending that inquest, but the coroner's office sent me everything that was said on DVD. Listening to it made just one thing clear: the investigation was a shambles.

DCI Jennings added: 'We believe it was very much a contract-style killing. It potentially may well have been a well-financed operation. It was very much a professional killing that could have taken weeks, if not months, of planning before it took place.'

To be honest, I could have told them that eighteen months earlier. It was also confirmed that John had been under surveillance since 2007.This just made it all the more astonishing. How on Earth could the police not have known more?

DCI Jennings at least had enough self-respect to admit there were 'failings on behalf of Essex Police'. Two police officers who had missed crucial signs that John was murdered had 'management action' taken against them for failing to properly inspect his body. But what was the entire team doing in that week before a Basildon Hospital pathologist inspected the body? It beggars belief how close we came to cremating his body without ever knowing what really happened to him.

Jennings said the timing of the killing played a large part in the ongoing investigation, but added: 'It may have taken weeks, if not months, of planning before it took place ... To be honest, we're no closer to finishing this inquiry.'

Christina and James did not attend the inquest either, which was surprising considering they had previously decided to help the BBC with a *Crimewatch* programme. Given the charges against her in Spain, I was amazed she agreed to take part.

'He had made mistakes in his life – I believe he has paid for those mistakes,' she told the programme. 'I was incredibly proud of the way he had adjusted to a very normal life.'

For me, this was hard to take. I was his real widow. The girls and I remained his family too, but we were being airbrushed out. It was all a bit rich to see Christina being depicted as the whiter-than-white victim in all this. And I certainly wouldn't have said John was living a 'normal' life. So much had happened to him that he remained paranoid about his safety. He always feared someone was out to get him, which is why he kept Rottweilers and covered his properties with CCTV. Clearly, his fears were not unfounded.

Despite almost thirty years of our love rivalry over John, Christina and I had only come face to face once, just three days after we were told John had been murdered. Sammy's partner, Steve, had set up the meeting, and convinced me it would be okay. I was hugely against the idea, but he told me it would be good for the girls.

'Christina is a nice woman,' he said. 'It will be worth it for all of you.' He was the only person who could have done that; I trusted and respected him. Steve is a lovely chap.

Christina and James were staying in a hotel at the time. Their vast home in Essex was being swarmed by forensic teams as police desperately attempted to make up for lost time.

After all those years, it was so weird to see my 'love rival' Christina get out of her car. She still had a full-time driver, and my daughters were in the back seats. Sammy, Janie and Steve had gone over to meet them in Essex before coming to me. James was not with them, probably because it would have made things even more complicated. This was about how things were shared on our side of the family. He wasn't relevant to our immediate lives.

We were all grieving, and now we had one hell of a mess to clean up. John's estate, or what was left of it, needed sorting before the vultures – the lawyers and accountants – swooped.

We decided it was best to have our dysfunctional family summit in Chapel Cottage, where Janie was still staying despite our legal fight.

I desperately tried to keep my nerves in check. I remember walking into the cottage, shaking like a leaf. I had spent so many years thinking about this woman, and what I might say to her. I never dreamt the circumstances would be as horrific as this.

As I arrived, she came in through the patio doors and stubbed out a cigarette she was sharing with Janie. 'Sorry, I've given up,' she said, her voice trembling.

Having previously seen a frumpy-looking woman on
TV, I was amazed by how chic she looked. She looked like
a businesswoman from a Next catalogue. She had a ponytail
and a smart trouser suit, with a floral pattern. I wouldn't have
blinked if someone told me she was a QC who had just come
out of court.

Sammy and Janie joined us inside. I noticed Christina was
shaking as much as me. We sat down on the settee, and my
daughters sat on two chairs opposite, in a square shape.

Christina broke the silence. 'John was larger than life, wasn't he?'

I nodded, and then noticed her shoulders drop, as though
she now felt she could relax. Christina spoke so differently
from me. She was almost reserved, very matter of fact and
measured with every sentence.

The calmer she seemed, the more emotional I felt. It made
me think how different we were. I am very direct, emotional
and instinctive, yet Christina was reserved, middle class and
cautious. She had a quiet charm about her, and I found her
quite likeable, but I couldn't help but think how extraordinary
it was that John had gone for her. Amazing that we were the
two loves of John's life.

Inevitably, the legal dispute over John's £800,000 demand
for our daughters came up.

She came straight out with it: 'What are you going to give
the girls? I know John wanted them to have that money.'

I couldn't believe what I was hearing. I looked at her
straight in the eye and gave her a taste of her own medicine.
'What are YOU going to give them? I know John would have
provided for them.'

'It's difficult for me,' she said. 'I've a lot of money problems.'

I had heard the rumours. I knew Christina was up to
her eyes in tax debt to the Spanish authorities. But equally,

Christina had taken it upon herself to be in charge of John's financial affairs. There was no denying, despite all the legal problems, that she was a very wealthy woman indeed.

Of course, I would want to help my own daughters. But at that point, with the house still up for sale, I had no liquid assets to share.

Fixing my stare on Christina again, taking in how smart and together she now seemed, I added, 'Surely John has looked after the girls in his will?'

'He didn't have one as he's a bankrupt,' she said.

If this was true, I knew he would have had another plan. He was constantly worried about being assassinated, and always told me James would look after Janie and Sammy if anything happened to him. In terms of financial help, there is no doubt he would have told Christina the girls needed to be looked after if he died.

Yet again, it didn't add up. John and I had our problems, but I knew he loved our daughters. All I had left was the property we had bought together and now his mistress, who had somehow taken on the whole fortune, was suggesting I should give up everything I had left to help the girls out. Of course, I would do what I could to help my own flesh and blood, but let's not kid a kidder: there must have been something hidden away that could be shared out.

The property in Bath was a drop in the ocean in terms of John's financial empire, even though much of it had been confiscated. Now he was gone, Christina could and should give my girls their fair share. I know that's what he would have wanted. For all his faults, he was always generous with money to those he loved. My girls worshipped him, and now I was being turned into the bad one by Christina, the one who had pulled this family apart in the first place.

Thankfully, our family summit at the cottage ended with no raised voices. There was even a kiss on the cheek as Christina and I said our goodbyes. I hope I never see her again, but I am glad that at least our one and only meeting was dignified.

You can imagine how surprised I was to read in *The Sun* a few months later that his will did in fact exist, but it had been frozen by Spanish authorities chasing their assets. 'Probate has been contested by authorities there who suspect the convicted timeshare fraudster kept running the scam from jail,' the report said.

Still to this day, the financial situation is a mess. Huge swathes of John's business interests were signed over to Christina over the previous decade. It was impossible for the creditors to work out who owned what. There was never a chance of me working out what was going on.

16

FALLOUT

As we approach three years since John's murder, I have given up on hope that the case will be solved. We can only come up with our own theories. So much of what we have been told by Essex Police has been hogwash.

The police were watching his every move in the months before he died. They really should have known more about his activities, his associates and his potential enemies. Officers have quizzed one of John's nephews and also one of his members of staff. To me, this is proof that officers are completely lost at sea. Whenever I have asked police about potential suspects, the only answer I get is: 'This is a very unusual case.'

Fat lot of good that is!

As the months went on and bore no fruit for the investigation, I began getting wild feelings that his death may have been faked or covered up in some way. It seemed impossible that the authorities could have mixed up the cause of death so dramatically. There were two different ambulances at the scene, as well as two police officers, his son and girlfriend. You would have been able to see the injuries clear as day.

It just seemed implausible. I kept asking the police, 'Is he definitely dead?'

Sammy and her boyfriend, Steve, eventually saw John at the morgue. I phoned Steve afterwards. He said he was sure the body was John, but even then I was still struggling to believe it all. The way John's life has been, I couldn't help but wonder whether all was not as it seemed. I even considered whether the head Sammy saw was a waxwork! Fanciful, I know, but we've all been to Madame Tussauds! These are the sort of paranoias you are wracked with in the dead of night where nothing makes sense. The whole case was so confusing.

The scene of the murder was simply too convenient. John was found in the only spot where he had not installed CCTV. And where were his dogs? It was virtually unheard of for him to keep his Rottweilers inside.

I think it's unlikely we will ever know the truth, but I can't help but think it's not beyond the realms of possibility that he did a deal with someone very powerful and he is on a sun-lounger somewhere, laughing at the lot of us!

There are so many possible outcomes but, by process of elimination, I think Hatton Garden has to be the most likely trigger for whatever happened. John was no grass. I am 100 per cent sure of that. He had no underworld connections by then. There would be nothing to tell police. I know that, but maybe others didn't. John knew everyone who was anyone in that world, and as he often told me: 'You can know too much.'

His powers were fading and, for most of his rivals, the value of killing him had diminished. Yet I can imagine why those involved in fencing loot from Hatton Garden would have wanted no stone unturned. The stakes were so high that summer.

John knew everyone in the jewellery business, both legit and black market. If, for example, the Hatton Garden gang had pinched one of his boxes, the industry would have known he would want revenge. And John may well have been able to work out who had been inside his box, long before the police. Leaving him alive may have been perceived as high risk. Worst of all, they might wrongly fear he would consider talking to police, bringing the whole deck of cards tumbling down. The underworld is a paranoid place. And when the gang discovered just a load of receipts and tapes, they would have realised they had no bargaining power with John. Of course, this is just wild speculation. But some sort of Hatton Garden link seems as likely as any other reason to pull the trigger on John.

Ultimately, though, it was the other great heist, Brink's-Mat, that set John on this path to a bloody end. He always said Brink's-Mat had changed everything for our lives. The wealth, pressure and fear warped his values. In his dogged pursuit of financial success, he destroyed our family, and his own happiness.

He got in over his head. He made stupid decisions, and became so obsessed by money that he believed he could buy himself out of any problems. Saskia, Christina, the drugs and the timeshares, in my opinion, were by-products of his disturbed mind and resentment.

*

I didn't go to John's funeral in the end, even though my youngest daughter begged me to join her. I hated to let her down, but I just knew it would be horrendous seeing everyone.

Christina and her son were the last people I would have wanted to see there. I think seeing James would break me.

John was besotted by his son. It would have brought up too much emotion. Instead, I said goodbye to him with my own little moment at home, without drama.

The funeral was in Brentwood. His brother Midge and sisters wanted him buried at a plot with the family in Birmingham. John's nephew, Darren Morris, who was due to face trial with his uncle and Christina, was also absent after being quizzed by police the previous day in connection with the murder. I don't think police ever seriously believed he was responsible – it was a strange move to swoop for him without any evidence.

John's ashes were eventually taken to Tenerife by Christina and my daughters. I was never consulted or invited to join the private ceremony. I probably would have turned down any invite, but it does hurt that I wasn't asked. They got on the *Brave Goose*, sailed out to sea and threw them in the water. A Viking burial of sorts. I think John would have liked that.

The loss and sadness of this whole sorry saga will never go away for me. John's influence still casts a shadow. Even in death he was still pulling the strings, manipulating my daughters into hating me.

When John died I thought it would end all that torment but the trouble he caused between me and my daughters over money is his way of haunting me from the grave. Now the girls perceive him as a martyr.

My daughters mean the world to me, but the hurt and damage feels irrevocable. It's deeply sad. The relationship between the three of us may never recover. My eldest daughter has only disdain for me. My youngest is just struggling to cope, and finds it impossible to keep in regular contact. I can't see things will ever be the same again for us.

'What have you done, John,' I think to myself. 'You're still causing pain and division. Is this your final cruel joke?'

The rift with my oldest daughter feels far beyond repair at the time of writing. Things are still very raw and we have both probably said things we regret. We were previously so close, and always looked after each other, all the way back to the fallout from Brink's-Mat. She is incredibly fiery, like her dad, but very vulnerable, like me. I'm told Janie is really struggling with life without him. I wish with all my heart that I could help her. All I want is to swoop in and help her get back on her feet. I just hope time heals us somehow, but I don't feel optimistic.

It may sound strange, but I have no regrets that I stood by John for so long. I would do it all again. There is no point in blaming him for everything. As he said, I was happy to take the good things. So often I believed he was an innocent bystander, always backing him, but ultimately he was never able to look after me and the girls in the way we needed because money was always more important.

Now, as I look back on my own life too, it is impossible to hate John. We loved each other, there's no two ways about it. He was, as Christina said, 'larger than life'. Had he kept on the straight and narrow, I've no doubt he would have been a huge success. John Palmer was a dealmaker extraordinaire and his charm lit up a room. In his own way, he cared for me, he loved his kids, and he was fond of Christina and his other lovers. But, ultimately, nobody came close to his love for cold hard cash.

My late husband's tragic circumstances were his choice. I don't look back on his life and think he was unfortunate. He chose to be domineering, controlling. He could have conquered his demons, but in the end they conquered him. Money was his biggest strength, and his biggest weakness.

★

Christina, I know, will be all right. She has a canny business brain, like John's. She has a host of limited companies, from gold dealing to antiques. These days, of course, it's all bought and sold online; some difference from our days sorting it all out in a bath and then flogging it out the back of a caravan at markets. The internet generation are probably making more money, but that's fine by me. I'd take a Lovejoy rogue over a Mark Zuckerberg geek every day of the week. I know who would be more fun.

However, I do wish John's 'second family' would do more for my daughters. Christina is now in charge of all of John's business interests. I know he would have wanted his daughters to have some financial security. Christina told me John hadn't left them anything. I still find that unbelievable. I would have liked to give them more out of my house sale, but I needed to find a roof over my head and there really wasn't much left after that. On Christina's side is the lot: Spanish villas, the *Brave Goose*, classic cars ... why can't my daughters have some of this?

Our divorce was only pending when he died. The last contracts were yet to be posted. I remain the real widow, and must pay the cost – in the eyes of the law, I remain the other half of a notorious fraudster. Suddenly credit cards get declined and you get warnings about bills. A couple of months ago, I phoned up to renew my home insurance. The vendor asked what my husband did, and when I told her he had been in prison, she doubled my premium. I have also been in touch with a solicitor about probate. The law firm made me fill out a security questionnaire and then refused to represent me because of John. Their letter said I am 'high risk through association'. Ridiculous!

There is no financial support to pay the bills. No widow's pension, and I have been forced to make some tough decisions.

Getting rid of the horses really broke my heart. They had kept me going. They were like family, and my time with them made me feel free of all the pain and anguish.

It's been a nightmare unravelling everything because we didn't even have his national insurance number. The police have been all over the place. 'It's strange – there doesn't seem to be one in existence for John,' the detective initially on the case said. Another officer shrugged his shoulders and said, 'It's very complicated because John never paid any tax.'

That's definitely not true. He paid less than he owed, sure, but I helped him write many of the cheques to the HMRC. They must have totalled a huge amount over the years.

Essex Police just never got a grip on anything around the case. They didn't even realise I was still married to John until I told them. A liaison officer from Avon and Somerset police came to visit me a few months into the investigation. It's fair to say he thought the investigation was a mess.

'You should ask some very searching questions, Marnie,' he told me.

He was right, but I'm now all but resigned to the depressing conclusion that we missed our only chance to catch John's killer in that lost week after the police's failure to spot he had been murdered. As time has gone on, the net has got wider. It's totally absurd that Essex Police would hint there are more than 16,000 people with motive to kill John.

I am still plagued by the dramas and torment of a lifetime with John Palmer. Clearly, I needed to move on and start looking after myself. The biggest first step was selling the Coach House. The first sale fell through, partly because John had neglected to get planning permission on much of the work he had done across the estate. The place was also falling apart around my ears because we had run out of cash for maintenance. We eventually exchanged contracts with another couple in the autumn of 2015 at a vastly reduced price. The buyers got an absolute bargain, but I was just glad to get out of there in the end. By January 2016, I was moving into my current home near Bath.

I have also found love again, with another John, and we have two lovely little Jack Russells, who we inherited when my stepdad died. My new John and I share a very different life. Much less drama, much more support. We don't get away nearly as much and the champagne doesn't flow quite at the same rate, but my little slice of normality is exactly what I need as I somehow try to repair.

My new man has changed my life. He makes me laugh and he listens and listens to all of my problems, when so many others turned their backs on me.

Angry letters still drop on my doormat, but life is really quite ordinary now. If some day you happen to pass me in the street or supermarket, you'll never guess I was Mrs Goldfinger!

Marnie Palmer
Near Bath
April 2018

GOLDFINGER
AND ME

BULLETS, BULLION AND BETRAYAL: JOHN PALMER'S TRUE STORY

MARNIE PALMER
WITH TOM MORGAN

This book is dedicated to my two daughters.
I love you both so much, and hope your
futures are much brighter and happier.

First published 2018

The History Press
The Mill, Brimscombe Port
Stroud, Gloucestershire, GL5 2QG
www.thehistorypress.co.uk

British Library Cataloguing in Publication Data.
A catalogue record for this book is available from the British Library.

ISBN 978 0 7509 8762 2

Typesetting and origination by The History Press
Printed and bound by CPI Group (UK) Ltd

THE APPEAL GOES ON ...

In June 2018, on the three year anniversary of Palmer's shooting, Christina's side of the family, with the support of Crimestoppers, offered a £100,000 reward for information leading to the arrest and conviction of his killer. DCI Stephen Jennings said he still believed it was a 'professional contract killing', adding that it was possible that three of the bullets were fired while Palmer was standing and three when he was on the ground. 'My belief is the person responsible in arranging this is someone very high up in the criminal underworld and we would expect if finances were used to purchase this killing you're talking about a large sum of money,' he said.

Detectives are continuing to appeal for information about a man and woman seen near Palmer's home the day before the murder. A man was also seen in Weald Country Park, next to Palmer's home, at 5.50 p.m. on the day he was shot. He was white, in his early 20s, around 5ft 10in and of slim build, with short, dark blond hair. He was wearing light blue jeans and a light-coloured baggy sweat top. Anyone who believes they have information about the murder of John Palmer is asked to call Essex police on 101 or Crimestoppers anonymously on 0800 555 111.

INDEX